CHANGING GEARS

CHANGING GEARS

DENISE REID

Library of Congress Control Number: 2020923482

ISBN:	Hardcover	978-1-5434-9696-3
	Softcover	978-1-5434-9697-0
	eBook	978-1-5434-9695-6

Print information available on the last page.

Rev. date: 03/03/2021

To order additional copies of this book, contact:
Xlibris
NZ TFN: 0800 008 756 (Toll Free inside the NZ)
NZ Local: 9-801 1905 (+64 9801 1905 from outside New Zealand)
www.Xlibris.co.nz
Orders@Xlibris.co.nz
815616

CONTENTS

LIST OF PICTURES

ACKNOWLEDGEMENTS

The scriptural basis of these studies are taken from the New International Version (NIV) of the Bible and the Amplified Bible. The New International Version Study Bible, Zondervan, Michigan, USA, 1978. The Amplified Bible, Zondervan, USA, 1965. Bible For Spirit Filled Living, New King James Version, Nelson, Nashville, USA, Parrican Standard Bible, Parsons Technology, Quick Verse Library, ISBN 9890-131-01-002. 1996.

Word meanings are taken from

Holman's Bible Dictionary, Parsons Technology, Quick Verse Library, ISBN 9890-131-01-002. 1996 Strong's Exhaustive Bible Concordance, James Strong, Holman Bible Publishers, Nashville, USA. ISBN 0-87981-626-0 1 984.

Collins Concise English Dictionary, Major New Edition, Glasgow, ISBN 000433160-5, 1988.

The Penguin Books, Penguin English Dictionary, Great Britain, Wyman, I Morehead, P., Roget's College Thesaurus, Signet, Chicago, USA, I

Readers Digest, Reverse Dictionary, Surrey Hills, NSW, 2010, 1996, ISBN 086449 0003.

Vine's Expository Dictionary of Old and New Testament Words, W. E. Vine, Vol.. A-Dys, page 335. & Vol. 4, Set – Z, page 165, 1981.

Parson's Technology, Quick Verse Library, Matthew Henry, Ryrie Study Bible, New American Standard Exhaustive Concordance, ISBN 9890-131-01-002. 1996

Anderson, K., Bold as a Lamb, Zondervan, Michigan, U.S.A. 1991. Hibbert, Albert, Smith Wigglesworth, The Secret of His Power, Harrison, Tulsa, USA.,

Meyer, Joyce, Battlefield of the Mind, Harrison House

TRIBUTES

To Jesus and to those who, over these years, have received amazing supernatural touches and seen supernatural events.

To my husband Kevin who has served and loved me. He has cherished, followed, facilitated, and empowered me through these years. He has worked, suffering with diligence and endurance. It is with his devotion, prayers, and help that the Lord has empowered me to undertake what together we have accomplished. To my husband Kevin, you are a true trojan and an extraordinary man of prayer. I celebrate you for your sacrifices.

To my daughter and son and my grandchildren who have lived sacrificially to release me to the purpose and plan of God.

To all those who have allowed their stories to be shared.

To my special friends and to the many nameless ones who have shared our lives and journeyed with me, changing gear to accelerate or slow down as necessary, and those who have gone on to their heavenly home and others.

To the many in the nations with whom we have worked, loved, and served, those we have watched grow mature and loved, who are family to us.

I want to thank Veruni Da Silva for the work she has done in design of the covers for this book.

Denise Reid

FOREWORD

A step into the unknown, wondering what I had let myself in for, as I did not know the ministry leader, just two of the team members.

A step into adventure, long flights train journeys. Travel by Jeep through wonderful scenery on the world's most dangerous roads in the Himalayan region to cities and small towns across India, Nepal, and Bhutan. A step into active faith and experiencing the glory of God.

As a team, we believed that we were being obedient to the will of God as he had spoken to us. God would fulfil all his promises to us as we taught the word and ministered to the people. Laying a good foundation, empowering them to kingdom living, by or through Holy Spirit gifts, and enabling them to do the works of Jesus. The word being evidenced by signs wonders and miracles.

"Faith looks at things a bit differently than reason as faith lives from the Unseen."

Denise is an inspiration in her fearless faith and in her experience of simply sharing the love of Jesus wherever she goes. An itinerant missionary who never knows what she might face, but her confidence is in God. When he calls her to do something, he backs her up all the way. Choosing to leave all old things behind, embracing change, and going forward, not quite knowing what's ahead. Bringing transforming truth and also practical aid to the people.

I encourage you to read this book with its powerful messages. You will be changed as you embrace the truths of these studies. As they have caused change and blessings to thousands of people across the nations where Denise and her teams have ministered. I have accompanied Denise on twenty missionary journeys and been privileged to be involved in the outpouring of Holy Spirit in times of tremendous breakthroughs. At times we saw something the Holy Spirit did, and we did not know at that time the scriptural bases for such events. They were there for searching and by revelation.

But, as it is written, "What no eye has seen, nor ear heard, nor the heart of man imagined, what God has prepared for those who love him" these things God has revealed to us through the Spirit. For the Spirit searches everything, even the depths of God. (ESV)

—1 Corinthians 2:9-10

Marian Mercer
Loved of God
New Zealand

ENDORSEMENT

I have known my dear friend Denise Reid for over twenty-five years.

We met at the Toronto Airport Church by a divine appointment, which I am sure we were not the only divine appointment God set up there over the years.

After a few days, I asked her to come to Seymour, Indiana, to minister; she accepted. That moment has developed into a great lasting relationship over the years.

I have traveled with her to Spain and Morocco, where God worked in marvelous ways.

Denise and Kevin have been frequent visitors in our home, which has given me opportunity to be able to speak about her love for the lost in the world and her passion to teach the fullness of the gospel of Jesus Christ.

Denise travels in faith with signs and wonders following. She is fearless and bold while the love of God flows through her.

This book is the story of what God can do through those who will step out in faith without looking back. She walks under the anointing of God to teach and preach the good news to the unreached of the world. But more than that, she takes you on a journey to heavenly places, and you don't leave your room. It will stir your spirit to get out of your comfortable room and go with her. She takes groups with her, so you can personally get involved in heavenly activities for yourself.

Reading this book should stir you up for an encounter with the same God she travels with. Expect the unexpected, be amazed by an amazing God, and go into the deep wells of anointing like never before as you read page by page.

Larry Robbins
Senior Minister, Seymour Harvest Church
Seymour, Indiana, USA

INTRODUCTION

Changing Gears is related to our journey on God's highway. Many people just want to slip to automatic. They think things will happen automatically. But we realise now that we need to progress through the driving. The key is to get a better performance out of a car, the same as with our walk with the Lord. We need to progress through the gears, and there are six of them: faith, obedience, relationship, vision, the anointing, and fire of God bringing the glory. Each one depends on the other. These are six gears taking us from plodding along, just plodding along, to a high speed on the king's highway.

This is a how-to book—how to drive, how to change gear, how to move forward, how to stop, how to think, how to pray, how to accelerate with faith, obedience, relationship, and vision and move in power. There's nothing instant here; microwave Christianity doesn't work.

People today want to go immediately to automatic. They don't want life on hold or pause; they want the microwave, which is automatic! But this is not about a microwave; this is a manual. They just want to push it into automatic and drive. In life, there are many people with no process, but progress is a process! There is a process in our walk with the Lord, and changing gears is a process.

Every time we move the car into gear, it changes the speed, changes the feel, changes everything. It's the same in our walk with Jesus. Changing gears moves us on. Faith and obedience moves on into relationship and vision. When we increase our relationship and vision, we move on. Every time we change gear, we depend on the past level, but we depend too on the new level, into which we want to be. Developing vision, we focus for the future level. All the previous gears are necessary for the final acceleration and overdrive. The exhilaration and excitement of the journey reveals itself as we settle in for the ride. Challenges of the power reach out and call to us to not pause and slow down but pause in his presence with ever growing intimacy of our relationship, ever-increasing faith and obedience as we trust him who made it all possible.

This is book three, written and published in a rapid release amidst Covid-19. When Covid hit, it stopped me. Time now to write as many people had spoken prophetically over the years. After thirty years of ministry, all travel ended. For thirty years, I travelled yearly around the world with no time to stop. Now with time to stop, I wrote. I sat down, recognised the timing, recognised the plan of God, recognised the purpose of God. I wrote. I wrote *Heavenly Kaleidoscope*, *Endless Safari* followed fast after, and now this third book, with the fourth in the plan! Now we're looking at a journey, changing gears. This is a journey into our walk with the Lord. Don't stay on pause, turn the key, put your foot down. We want to move into acceleration, high speed, a green light where nothing stops us. Acceleration in purpose, acceleration in the plan, and excitement in the journey as we sit back, listen to the Lord, and rest in his purpose.

Some substance in this journey results from material shared during twenty-fours of seminars in Nepal. It has developed from experiences in the restricted nations where persecution has lit revival fires. The churches in nations such as Russia, Bulgaria, Cuba, and Asia purified through the fires of persecution, have experienced glorious outpourings of the Holy Spirit. As with the other books, I have shared many experiences from these nations. I have changed names to protect the people whose stories I have shared.

While ministering at Snell's Beach Baptist Church in New Zealand, I noticed an Asian man listening attentively. Afterwards, he came to me and said, "You must come to Nepal!"

I replied, "Look, it's impossible. Nepal had been on my heart for three years, and I thought I would go this year, but I am going to all these other countries, and Kevin will be unhappy if I extend the trip to go further."

He replied, "You are already going to Myanmar, and it's only a little more cost to go on to Nepal!" He said, "God told me to come here today and ask you to come to Nepal!"

I replied, "Well, speak to Kevin."

As a result, I took a team of two other ladies, one of whom was my daughter, and we travelled to Russia, Bulgaria, Myanmar with finally twelve days in Nepal at a training centre.

We arrived with instructions that we would minister to village ladies for a few hours each day. I had given away most of my notes and materials in Bulgaria and Russia, as the need for teaching materials is desperate in these nations. When we settled at the leader's house, he said, "For five days, you have four hours each day teaching in the Bible school!"

It was wonderful what God did as he changed and transformed lives. There were twenty-one evangelists-pastors, two of whom were illiterate, and some of whom lived in caves. As every day we ministered by the word and in action, we saw them come from darkness to light. We saw them delivered and set free, and finally, on the second to the last day, they all came into a fresh experience of the Holy Spirit.

NEPAL STUDENTS

This book is written and dedicated to all those who sincerely desire to know God more, how to move by faith into the anointing and power of God. The material shared about the fire of God and the glory of God comes from research for ministry in these areas, personal experiences, and precious times spent in churches where persecution has lit revival fires.

It is my prayer that as you read these pages, they will assist you to walk as Jesus walked in power, love, and mercy with an ever-deepening relationship to his word and his will. I pray that you will arise and do the works that Jesus did and see his glory fall as the fire of God comes in answer to your surrendered life.

Over these past thirty years, because of the first trip to Asia, in obedience to the word of the Lord, we have taken many teams to change the lives of thousands. That trip in the temples in Myanmar, I had a revelation of God. I saw there was no other name given under heaven whereby salvation would come to men and women. It was only at the name of Jesus, through the power of the blood of Jesus, that hope would come to a hopeless world. It's been and is an endless safari of changing gears, listening to and obeying the Lord. Without Christ, many are in the valley of decision. Who will tell them of Jesus's love?

SCHWEDAGON PAGODA

It's harvest time. Right now, the harvest of the earth is ripe. Will you take the sickle and reap? Will you share the good news of the gospel? The harvest is white; the labourers are few. How can they hear without a preacher?

DENISE REID

HOW TO MOVE OUT OF NEUTRAL, OUT OF PARK

HOW TO MOVE INTO FAITH

Our lives have been about seeing, saying, and doing! For thirty years, we have travelled the world, living by faith, not taking a salary, trusting God for our needs and needs in the nations. Faith is the how to just do it, and that is what we have done for more than thirty years! Faith comes from knowing more of God each day.

Smith Wigglesworth, that great faith preacher, would say, "Faith comes by hearing, and hearing by the Word of God, not by reading commentaries. Faith is the principle of the word of God. The Holy Spirit, who inspired the Word, is called the Spirit of Truth; and as we receive with meekness the engrafted Word, faith springs up in our hearts" (Hibbert 1982).

THE HOW-TO OF FAITH

Faith comprises three things: Believe the facts, obey the commands, enjoy the promises; seeing, saying, and doing. Genesis 1 is the how-to of God—how to see, how to say, and how to do. God said it, he saw it, and it was so —it happened!

Are you crazy enough just to do what God says? Faith comprises of how to do the crazy thing—to believe God and do it—to enjoy the results. When you get in a new or different car, get used to the model, learn and gain confidence. Faith is about learning who you are and having and increasing in confidence to move ahead.

It all began in 1989, during an Armed and Dangerous Seminar. The theme featured "Whatever God Speaks to You About, Do It." Until then, I had been just an ordinary, boring New Zealand Christian. At the church, during the singing of a dull old hymn, God spoke and told me to go to Myanmar. I had never been out of New Zealand and did not have a passport, but I contacted a mission organisation that I knew planned to send a team. When I told my husband, he amazed me, for he strongly encouraged me to go, as I had expected he would say, 'impossible!'

As I confessed I would go to Myanmar, I held fast to the word of God. Now I praised God and declared that he would fulfil his word, for I had faith in God. Yet I moved out of drive, out of neutral into engagement, engagement with God, engagement into faith as the gear, the how to, to bring change.

Jesus never fails, for faith changes things. My faith appeared to be on the line as I spoke to the mountain of obstacles. I worked full time and could not get the time off. My immediate supervisor granted the leave but later withdrew it. Finally, I visited the principal of the polytechnic and explained that I had an opportunity to travel overseas. As I had never been before, I asked him to grant me special leave. As it was now against policy, he invited me back three times to discuss the matter and kept on saying he did not want me to lose any money. As the deadline for the ticket purchase came, again, I visited him, but he could not decide. Now I felt to tell him the real reason I wanted to go. Wide-eyed and almost open-mouthed, he said to me, "But Myanmar is communist. What you are going to do, taking Bibles, is illegal! You could go to prison!"

I said, "Definitely, but God is looking after me."

I am convinced that I will return. He told me he admired what I wanted to do and would I please give him a further twenty-four hours to decide. The next day at 12:15 p.m., the telephone in my office rang.

"This is the principal," the voice said. "I grant your leave."

To make sure I had heard him correctly, I repeated the statement.

"That is correct," he said.

After thanking him, I replaced the receiver, praising God who answers active believing faith, who acts on behalf of those who wait on him. Six weeks later, after seeing many miracles of faith and with his encouragement, with the team of fourteen others, we embarked on a trip that changed my life. It was the how-to—how to start doing what I would always do for the rest of my life!

KEVIN AND DENISE

FAITH BRINGS OBEDIENCE. FAITH IS NOT FAITH UNTIL IT IS ALL YOU HAVE TO HOLD ON TO.

THE HOW-TO OF FUTURE ACTION, THE KEY THAT UNLOCKS THE DOOR

KNOWLEDGE + OBEDIENCE = FAITH

GREAT FIGHTS PRODUCE GREAT FAITH.

This became a fight of faith, even a challenge to greater relationship, a challenge to change. With a world map on our wall, I spoke daily, saw into the unseen, and declared into being the vision by faith. Yet a great fight it became. First, for the leave to be granted; next, for the passport and renewal of the mislaid marriage licence and all details to come forth. And all achieved in six weeks in time to fly with the team! A learning curve of moving from shaky, limited belief to active faith.

Faith comes by hearing, hearing by the word of God, learning what to do. Turn the key before the gears work to take us forward! To learn to turn the key to new action became crucial to this new journey.

Faith is from the Greek *pistis*, *pisteno*, *peitho*, which means to agree, have confidence to assent to, a firm persuasion, moral conviction of religious truth or the truthfulness of God or a religious teacher with reliance upon Christ for salvation.

> No unbelief made him waver concerning the promise of God, but he grew strong in his faith as he gave glory to God . . .
> —Romans 4:20 ESV

It says, "He did not waver through unbelief regarding the promises of God but was strengthened in his faith. And gave the glory to God." Abraham's faith convinced him that God would do what he promised. "Faith brings glory to God." Abraham's faith, credited to him as righteousness, turned out to be true faith. He had complete confidence in God's promises. He called the things that were not as if they are. This is a principle of the word of God. Yet strong in his faith, he had been strengthened as his faith gained ground by exercise. And he grew strong, empowered by faith, as he gave praise and glory to God.

We are to see with the eyes of faith, to look beyond what we can see in the natural, to what God will do, at what he already has done, but we are not yet seeing. Faith does not refuse to face reality but looks beyond all the difficulties to God and his promises. This is not presumption but living faith. It's not enough to just trust.

Romans 4:21 (ESV) says faith looks past the problems to the fulfilment of the promise. Abraham found how to stand and act on God's word. He staggered not at God's promise. Fully persuaded, Abraham had no previous knowledge nor evidence that God could raise the dead. It had never happened before, yet he became certain he would do it (Genesis 22:5 ESV).

Faith fastens on God. It is God who delights to do the impossible. The word of God says, "I am the God of the impossible" (Luke 1:37 ESV). Abraham turned out to be strong in faith.

When God intends some special blessing for his people, he puts a sentence of death upon the blessing itself. Again, this is a principle of the word of God. God brought life to the dead. Abraham's body looked as good as dead. God empowered him to accept, enabled hope to come forth, arising out of God's all-sufficiency (Genesis 22:1-10 ESV, Romans 4 ESV). The child came to be born because they activated faith (Genesis 13:14, 17:15-22 ESV).

Faith always says, "It's mine! I have it now!" Faith never looks back. Abraham's faith gave glory to God. God gives honour to faith because faith gives honour to God (2 Corinthians 4:18 ESV) as we look not to the things that are seen but to the things that are unseen. For the things that are seen are transient, but the things that are unseen are eternal.

(TPT) because we don't focus our attention on what is seen but on what is unseen. What is seen is temporary, but the unseen realm is eternal. I called it mine! When I wavered and faltered looking at the circumstances, Kevin encouraged me, even when it appeared impossible. Together, we stood on the word of God, depending on the God of the word.

Abraham staggered not through unbelief, even when God told him to take his son, his only son. After he obeyed, with blind faith, he saw that God must resolve this problem, even if he had to raise Isaac from the dead. Yet told to kill Isaac, he planned to do it! He accepted without question (Genesis 22, Hebrews 11:19 ESV).

What a test! How would we respond? This son, about whom he had such promises to be the seed of many nations. Look at Genesis 22:5 (ESV) and his faith. He said to the servants, "Stay here—until I and the boy come back to you."

Yet he understood and trusted the word of God, even when tested in this way. Abraham hoped against hope (Hebrews 11:19 ESV). He said, "I hope so" and "I believe so"; therefore, "I know so." We must do so too!

Absolutely no hesitation, not an argument, nor a debate or self-consultation, and no procrastination. What an example for us!

FIRST TEAM TO MYANMAR

In Genesis 22:10 (ESV), it says he took the knife, and he raised it to slay the boy, his son, bound to the altar, waiting for that knife to descend! But God answered believing, active faith; God provided a ram!

> And whatever you shall ask for in prayer, having faith and really believing, you shall receive . . .
> (—Matthew 21:22 ESV)

When we do not know what to do, we are in a good place. Before God tried him, Abraham could not offer Isaac. Called the father of the faithful, he would not give up under trials. As he learnt through adverse circumstances, trials, and difficulties, he understood the faithfulness of God.

And it reminds me of a famous pastor in Asia, who shows us entire trust in God. While very young and poor, he prayed for a chair, a bicycle, and a table. He declared, he decreed, and he prayed, knowing God would do it. When he asked God for the chair, bicycle, and table, he waited and waited, but nothing happened. At church, he declared he had a chair, a bicycle, and a table. They, the elders, the people, came to look. When he opened his door, they came in the room eager to spot his chair, bicycle, and table! But they saw nothing, and puzzled, they asked, "Pastor, where is your chair, where is your bicycle, and where is your table?"

He replied, "Can you behold the chair, the table, the bicycle? No! When a woman is pregnant, it takes nine months for the baby to come! You see evidence of the baby, but no baby. Then comes the delivery, and there is the baby! I am pregnant with, I am trusting God for the chair, the bicycle, and the table, and I am pregnant with them until they come. They are growing within me."

The people laughed and laughed. They understood what he said, and they left smiling, saying, "Our pastor is pregnant and one day will have a chair, a bicycle, and a table."

He trusted God, and sometime later he received the chair, the bicycle, and the table. He had no doubt of God's faithfulness. We are to learn from this example and have no doubt of God's faithfulness.

In Myanmar, my friend Brother Ray shared that in the country's north lived a pastor who owned a bull. Because the bull was a prized possession, he put a bell around its neck. This meant he always knew where the bull was and how to find the bull. One day he could not hear the tinkle, tinkle of the bell. Now he worried as he could not find the bull. It had vanished. As he listened to Christian programmes on the radio from Far East Broadcasting, he learnt God cared about him. He heard about a God who answers prayer, and he prayed to the God of the radio and said, "God of the radio, if you are there, please find my bull."

Yet all day he looked for his bull but could not find the bull. Now anxious, he knew, if he did not find it by dark, the bull would be meat by morning! He kept on asking God to help. After dark, late that night, at almost midnight, he heard a sound he had been longing for. *Tinkle, tinkle, tinkle, tinkle, tinkle, tinkle.* Nearer and nearer it came. Then it stopped. He hurried outside onto the landing, and there came his bull! He gave thanks and praise to the God of the radio!

BROTHER RAY

When we know more of God, each day faith comes. God wants us to come into that place where we will never look back because he knows when we do so, we go back. God has no room for someone who looks back, thinks back, or acts back. He wants us every day to be in a rising tide with ever-changing faith (Wigglesworth).

The living word of God is the only foundation for faith. We are to have faith in the integrity of the word of God and not require any other evidence. However, we often require evidence before we believe. But with trust in God, we place confidence in him until we have it! Yet that is what our friend in Asia did. When the word of God fills our heart, there is the force of faith. When we speak, we hear, conviction comes based upon hearing, and we profess what we hear.

We have a firm conviction that produces a full acknowledgement of God's revelation or truth. This brings personal surrender, and we yield to him and produces conduct inspired by such surrender. (Strong's Exhaustive Concordance - Vine's Concordance.)

Other words we associate with faith are *belief* and *trust.*

Do you know that chorus, "Only believe, only believe, all things are possible, only believe" (Mark 5:36 (ESV), Paul Rader 1921)

I have been learning from the example of the man Smith Wigglesworth, who said, "I am not moved by what I see, I am moved only by what I believe." Moved by the winds and waves, Peter began to sink. He forgot to trust Jesus (Matthew 14:30 KJV). Things are never as they appear (1 Samuel 17:11, 24 KJV). The Israelites were dismayed and terrified at what they saw and heeded.

Just accept that God is greater than you are, greater than your heart, greater than your thoughts. Only then can he establish us in righteousness. If we will just declare and decree the word, the devil will not cope with us! God is looking for someone who will just have no doubt!

I understood that the Bible message about faith began with Abraham, the great man of faith. But God revealed that is incorrect, and Genesis began it. With revelation, I saw faith started in Genesis 1, when God created the world. And John 1 says God spoke, and his words formed the world. In the beginning was the word, and the word was God. Let's consider creation, when God acted.

We find in Genesis 1 ESV three principles of faith. In verse 3, it says God said; in verse 4, it says God saw; and in verse 5, it happened. Faith begins with God. He caused to exist that which had no previous being.

In Genesis 1:3 (ESV), God spoke by faith. He said, "Let there be light," and light came. He called the unseen into being. He decreed the light by faith and declared it into being. In verses 3, 4, and 5, it says, and

God said it, and then God saw it, and it was so! The elements had to obey him. The word of God framed the world. These are the principles of acting, believing faith. God painted a picture with his words; he framed the inner image of the universe with words. Then he released words filled with faith. Through the power in the words, he brought into manifestation the picture the words painted.

God spoke the word. After he trusted the word, he gazed with the eyes of faith. He said, in verse 3, "Let there be light," and in verse 6, "Let there be," and it happened because he expected something to happen. When the elements obeyed him, they recognised his authority, and God beheld the results. When God speaks, the same power is available to us. God spoke the world into being. Seven times he spoke. This is the number of perfection, to which nothing can be added. This is an example for us to follow, we should follow. God spoke the elements into being seven times. If God can do it, so can we.

As faith acts, it becomes a reality, a deposit of God, an almighty flame moving you to act so that signs and wonders are manifest. Faith is laying hold of the unrealities of hope and bringing them into the realm of reality by acting on the word. Faith is a servant; we must put it to work.

Hebrews 11:1 (ESV) says Now faith is the assurance of things hoped for, the conviction of things not seen.

Faith is the heavenly substance of what you desire in your heart, heaven's part of you, a spiritual force, God's creative power. Now faith is the confident taking of what God offers. Hope is expecting a future blessing. There is the favorable confident expectation, the eager longing, the certainty of producing action. Hope that is seen is no hope at all. Who hopes for what he already has?

Yes, we are to be sure of what we hope for, trusting what we hear from the Bible, being certain of what we cannot gaze upon. Yet the world says,

"I hope so," "I wish so. I must glimpse it to accept it." But the Bible says, we know so and that we call it into being until we have it.

Doers fill the church, people who are busy, busy, busy doing! Not believers who stand on the word and accept the word. Peter's actions showed him to be a doer; John's showed him to be a believer. Trust God can change you, accept God can heal, know he loves you. Just be bold, take him at his word.

> Hope deferred makes the heart sick.
> (—Proverbs 13:12 ESV)

When we only hope and it does not happen, disappointment arises, and we die to the dream!

"For faith is the very nature of God, the personal inward flow of the Divine favor. Faith is the glory of His presence within us, changing us from glory to glory, from strength to strength until we are like Enoch who God spoke through," (Jude 1:14; ESV Hebrews 11:5 ESV).

And faith is now; if it is not now, it is not faith! The principles of faith are unchanging. We receive Jesus by faith; we receive the Holy Spirit by faith.

Faith changes things. When the men took the paralytic man and lowered him down through the roof to Jesus, their faith moved him, and their confidence in God grew through him (Mark 2:5 ESV). They knew Jesus would heal him. God says he will bless us if we move by faith.

When we left New Zealand with $800 and round-the-world tickets, we moved by faith, and God blessed and provided our every need.

Our ministry is a ministry of faith; as by faith, people go on teams, and by faith, we accept them. By faith, we lay hands on the sick, and it heals people. I would never have dreamt that I would travel the world for thirty years except by faith. As every year we travel the world, we are convinced of God, convinced of active believing faith. The money hasn't been there, but God has provided as we looked to him.

"By grace through faith," not just through faith Ephesians 2:8 (KJV)

Grace is the power of God that comes to me through the channel of my faith to get the job done. Wigglesworth said, "Faith is not the price to buy it, but the hand that receives the blessings." Grace is of God. It is by faith. You open the door by faith, and God comes.

Faith is the power of access; faith that never has a mixture in with all that you want, faith that never wavers, faith that is audacious, faith that is pure, faith sensitive to the breath of God, faith that is the very nature of the Son of God, faith that comes from the author of faith. Jesus, "the author and finisher (perfector) of faith," gives us this faith (Hebrews 12:3 ESV).

Ephesians 3:20 (TPT) says *never doubt* God's mighty power to work in you and accomplish all this. He will achieve infinitely more than your greatest request, your most unbelievable dream, and exceed your wildest imagination! He will outdo them all, for his miraculous power constantly energises you.

When we understand this, we can have more, much more, than we can ever imagine according to his power. As our confidence in God increases, we refuse to accept a reason to doubt. Faith is not the product of reason; it is the product of the recreated spirit. Complete trust and confidence in God creates an environment for miracles. It is a seed, with the natural power of a seed (Mark 4:20 ESV, Genesis 8:22 ESV). When we consider a seed of corn, it is planted and nurtured and grows to produce a cob of corn. It won't produce an apple. Genetically, it reproduces after its own kind and produces a harvest. For us, it is the same, as faith begets faith. We speak the word of God, and it becomes alive and active in our lives, and our faith grows. Confession brings possession.

AN EXAMPLE OF FAITH IS ABRAHAM

Abraham, the man of faith, is our father, the father of faith. There is a new race from Abraham. Genesis 12:1-4 (ESV) speaks of Abraham. God promises to make Abraham great. As a wealthy man, he risked all to follow God into the unknown, leaving family, friends, and everything familiar to him. He did not go in blind faith, but in complete confidence in God's utter trustworthiness. His faith expressed itself in obedience. He did not know where his journey would go. He received the promise by faith, not through law, but by trusting God. Abraham pleased God by leaving his own country, his friends, everything familiar to him. He obeyed God's command. Faith fastens upon God, what God can do because of faith. The God of glory appeared to him (Acts 7:2). His faith pleased God (Hebrews 11:6 ESV).

We are to be certain, and then we receive. Believing is an action word. Rest assured this is acting on the word. Placing confidence in the word of God and acting upon it will cause results to happen (Mark 11:24 ESV). We have to know it is impossible for God to break his word because he is from everlasting to everlasting.

> I believed and therefore have I spoken.
> (—2 Corinthians 4:13 ESV)

FEATURES OF THE LIFE OF ABRAHAM

Abraham's faith mused on nothing but the faithfulness of the promise, and this strengthened him and kept up his faith. He did not waver or gaze at the difficulties. Is fulfilled spelt wrongly?

He committed everything to realise the promise fulfilled. Abraham became the father of many nations.

God spoke a new name to Abram. The Lord arranged it so that every time Abraham spoke his new name or someone called him Abraham, he would remember God's promise, and his faith would activate. Abraham placed confidence in hope, and he had hope that God would do what he said, give him a son (Genesis 12:2 ESV). He knew that God could make his heirs like the stars in the sky (Genesis 13:14 ESV), that he would make him the father of many nations and bless the nations through him (Genesis 12:2-4, 17:3, 22:17 ESV).

> That is why it depends on faith, in order that the promise may rest on grace and be guaranteed to all his offspring—not only to the adherent of the law but also to the one who shares the faith of Abraham, who is the father of us all . . .
> (—Romans 4:16-17 ESV)

As it is written, "I have made you the father of many nations"—in the presence of the God in whom he believed, who gives life to the dead and calls into existence the things that do not exist.

It is the outcome of faith. Our inheritance depends upon faith. This means we can open the door and God will come in. Abraham learnt to act like God and speak of the things that are not as though they were (Ephesians 5:1 ESV, Galatians 4:29 ESV).

Romans 4:17-20 (ESV) says, "The God who gives life to the dead and calls the things that are not as if they were." This is past tense, where God enabled him to behold the total impossibility. "Against all hope Abraham in hope glimpsed God's purpose and so became the father of many nations. Without weakening in faith, he faced the fact that his body, though as good as dead, could live. And when absolutely persuaded, he knew God could do as He promised." He had tried everything, but God came, and then came hope. We are to stay in the word until it becomes the word of God to us.

> By faith Abraham when called to go, journeyed to a place he would later receive as an inheritance.
> (—Hebrews 11:8 ESV)

He obeyed, trusting God would go with him and would fulfil his word to him, and he travelled into the unknown. Yes, he journeyed forth to possess an inheritance by faith. He didn't know what the future held or the journey ahead of him. Abraham and his offspring received the promise by faith, not through the law, but by trusting God. At seventy-five years old, when God spoke, what could God do as the result of such faith? He could bring life to the dead. Sarah was ninety-five and Abraham was one hundred years old when they conceived Isaac. Yes, an impossible situation. They were both past thc ycars of childbearing. Old, finished, only God could breathe life into these dry bones! With no heir, a hopeless situation. The Bible records her as having said, "Can I have such pleasure at my age?" and she even laughed at the impossibility! Persuaded, the word came between him and God, just as the blood of Jesus is between us and God. He hoped, then faith came, then Isaac! A covenant was between him and God as blood stood between him and God.

When we pray, in heaven it is already done, and we await the manifestation. We have to peer with the eyes of faith. Abraham did not consider his own body which was as good as dead.

In 1990, on my second ministry trip, I travelled for six weeks to Asia. As I prayed by faith and spoke God's word over my life, there were many obstacles. No money, no one with whom to travel. They cancelled the leave granted to me, but God came through. Again, I visited the principal of the polytechnic (where I worked). I spoke with eyes of faith, and it happened. When I prayed for a companion, God sent a woman from Britain to meet me in Bangkok to go with me to Myanmar. God is faithful. While in Thailand, I phoned New Zealand to discover that money had come in to pay all expenses. Praise his holy name!

Our confession if only mental will soon fail. When we fill our hearts with the word, we change the atmosphere over our lives.

JANE

WE CAN HAVE THE FAITH THAT PLEASES GOD

Let us learn to speak of things that are not as though they are (Romans 4:17, Isaiah 48:13, Genesis 17:5 ESV).

We are not to consider our bodies or any surrounding circumstances. Yet we are to stagger not at God's promises (Romans 4:20 ESV). We are to be certain God will perform his word.

When I had cancer, the doctors spoke of death at every stage. But I believed God spoke life over my life and trusted the word. Because of the radiation, my shoulder froze and would not move. Yet I lay on the floor, every day exercising and forcing it to move. As I declared the promises of God that he healed me, that I would go to Cuba, that my shoulder would move, he did! God healed it. Cancer never returned.

Jesus marveled at the faith of the centurion. He had faith in the integrity of the word of Jesus, the word of God, and did not require any other evidence. Notice that he did not even pray! Neither Jesus nor the centurion prayed!

We are to have no doubt in the authority of God's word. In the name of Jesus, he has given us as believers the right to the fullness of his word.

> So that the tested genuineness of your faith —more precious than gold that perishes though it is tested by fire—may be found to result in praise and glory and honour at the revelation of Jesus Christ.
> (—1 Peter 1:7 ESV)

Gold perishes, but faith never perishes.

In James 2:22-23 (ESV), you see that faith, along with his works, was active. Faith was completed by his works and the scripture was fulfiled. "Abraham believed God, and it was counted to him as righteousness"—and he was called a friend of God.

Yet Abraham's faith was completed by his actions, as it acted. His faith and his actions worked together. We must act on the word. Healed people should act healed. While in Cuba, we prayed for a crippled man who walked without his cane. Though he rejoiced at his healing, he picked up the cane, saying he might need it. While Abraham acted on the truth of the word, we must do so too. So many people lose their trust just as this man did, and the result is they then lose their healing!

When we are born again, the spirit of God imparts faith to act without doubt or fear. As it's a heavenly substance, a gift that comes through the spirit of the Lord, we cannot conjure it up. It comes as we surrender to the spirit of the Lord. It's not our faith, it's his, and we birth it. Faith becomes a part of you. Since it's so simple, we have nothing to do with it; if we did, we would take the glory. But faith gives the glory to God because God does it.

Since God keeps us in that faith, it requires us to follow. God works it in, I work it out, and as I work it out, it grows. Now we do not produce or conjure it up; it comes when we surrender to the spirit of the Lord. As long as we make the choice every day to live by our senses, we do not live by faith.

We can place confidence in the invisible things of God or trust in the natural realm, the things we see, touch, and discern. They depend on our logic and reason, our natural mind, but we are to order our lives by what God says is true. Faith always comes before feeling; it does not depend on how we sense something. Since feelings come and feelings go, we never doubt that God and his word are unchanging.

The realm of the natural, material world binds the person without faith to what's possible and places them in the same position as in the animal kingdom. David fought and conquered the lion and the bear by the strength of the Lord (1 Samuel 17:34 ESV). Until we speak to the natural world, we cannot see the desired results (Mark 4:39, Luke 17:5-6 ESV). God intended for us to exercise authority over the world and all he created.

1 Corinthians 2:6-16, (ESV) for faith to grow and take dominion we must follow the rules. Though the five senses give information, we are not to live in the reasoning realm but to live in the realm of revelation, verse 12.

God's ways are higher than our ways. Man stood to have dominion over all things on earth. With the fall of Adam, man lost this (Genesis 1:26-31, Genesis 3, Isaiah 55:8-11 ESV). As God's word will accomplish and achieve, it will not be without effect. Jesus used God's way of dominion. In Mark 1:40-42 (ESV), Jesus's word instantly cured the leper and made him clean. In Luke 13:10-13 (ESV), Jesus's word instantly healed the woman bent over with a spirit of infirmity. When we are born again, we become a new creation and receive the life of Christ. We are restored to rule and reign, as in Genesis 1, to have dominion!

As faith in Jesus Christ gives us access to the fullness of God, we will receive like precious faith. Since we receive faith like Jesus, faith like the apostles, we can do what they did (Hebrews 11:33; 2 Peter 1:11 ESV).

In Mark 11:12-26 (ESV), Jesus says, have faith in God or have the faith of God. After we have the God kind of faith, we can speak to situations! When Jesus spoke to the fig tree, it withered from the top down. He did not look for the change as he did not have to perceive it. As long as we impart faith, we recognise we have the faith of God. Jesus said, "Do you have the faith of God?" This implies it must be possible. We are to have it. It's a possibility. Though the Greek rendering is to have the faith of God, how can we have God's faith? Well, we can't because God has the faith and imparts faith. Yet you have the faith of God; you received his faith when you were born again.

Faith is spiritual, and belief is mental. Since we can give mental assent to things while doing nothing, we have a problem. But we are to have the faith of God, and God's faith is active. As mental assent is worth nothing and does nothing, we must speak, act, give credence to, and forgive. In absolute trust, we must follow the instructions and do what they say.

As "I hope so" is not enough, we must know so and we must act. Whenever we follow the instructions and do what they say, we see fulfilment of what it says. He shall have whatever he says. For we are to speak, to act, and to accept with no doubt. As we recognise God spoke it, we affirm it happened. The Bible is the instruction book, a how-to, and we are to do what it says. When we have a recipe, we follow the recipe.

While faith always involves significant risk, the rewards are great.

James 1:6-7 Just make sure you ask empowered by confident faith without doubting that you will receive. For the ambivalent person believes one minute and doubts the next. Being undecided makes you become like the rough seas driven and tossed by the wind. You're up one minute and tossed down the next.

[TPT]

Don't fool yourself, you will get nothing; what you confess controls you. If you are saying, "O God, I hope so," flag it!

So also faith by itself; if it does not have works, it is dead.

But someone will say, "You have faith, and I have works."

Show me your faith apart from your works, and I will show you my faith by my works (James 2:17-20 ESV). After we trust implicitly, God goes to work, as belief is not enough. You believe that God is one; you do well. Even the demons believe—and shudder!

Do you want to be shown, you foolish person, that faith apart from works is useless?

When we don't act on what we accept and understand, our faith is worth nothing. We can't just be certain of; we must act, move in by faith, then God will do it. When God spoke, the elements obeyed. The demons will obey and recognise our authority.

Act, speak to the mountain, tell it to go!
(—Mark 11:23 ESV)

While faith is believing we have what God says we have, we act accordingly before we grasp or recognise we have it. We must speak what the word says. If we want power and authority, we must agree with the word. The demons respond to our authority if we attach weight to and act on the word. We must do more than hope so.

Matthew 12:34-37 (ESV) says, "Out of the overflow of the heart the mouth speaks, He shall have whatsoever he saith." Whatever a person says reveals what is in their heart. Our confession is what we are, and if we say we are weak, that is what we are—WEAK. And if we say we are sick, that is what we are—SICK. Out of the heart, the mouth speaks, and by our words, we will be acquitted or condemned. And according to our faith, it will be for us (Mark 11:22, Matthew 21:22 ESV).

When we continue to be convinced and praise him for what he has given, we don't depend on what we examine; we presume true what he says. This reveals what is in our heart. We continue to have no doubt until we behold it because after we conclude its truth, God goes to work.

GOD'S WORD IS FAITH'S FOUNDATION

> Do not let my word depart from your mouth, meditate on it day and night.
> (—Joshua 1:8 ESV)

For meditation on the word brings the inner image of what and who we are in Christ Jesus.

> Those who know your name will trust in you.
> (—Psalm 9:10 ESV)

As we trust God, trust that he always acts according to the word. We choose to accept the Lord will never forsake us when we trust in him.

Psalm 37:5 (ESV) says we are to commit our way daily to the Lord. Daily I ask the Lord to be with me, to watch over me, as I yield my life to him.

Psalm 43:3 (ESV), Psalm 119:105 says, "God's word is a light, a lamp to our feet and to our path." "Send forth your light and your truth.

Once we expect God's spirit to bring light in the Scriptures he speaks and guides us every day."

He brings light to our path. When God spoke, telling me to go to the USA, I believed him, and he brought light to our path. When I declared and spoke over the map of the world that I would go to nations, it happened. When I spoke that miracles, signs, and wonders would happen, they happened. As I declared over people that Jesus healed them, he healed them, even when I didn't know what the problem could be.

Psalm 46:7 (ESV) says we are the mouthpiece of God. As the word of God takes first place in our lives, we become the mouthpiece of God. "The God of Jacob is with us, He is our fortress."

In Psalm 51:10 (ESV), when we ask God to create in us a pure heart and to renew a steadfast spirit within us, he does it. A spirit that is single-minded stands strong, keeps going, and stands firm on the truth. As we act focused and single-minded, God acts in ways we could never dream, expect or ask!

When Maury, a team member in Nepal, laid hands on a man with a distorted face, he watched that face return to almost normal. The next day that man testified of his healing.

MAURY [RIGHT] BESIDE DANI AND BEVAN DOING DRAMA

Psalm 55:22 (ESV) says we trust God by casting our cares upon him. After I slipped and slid on the ice, which ruptured the muscle in my leg, I fell down two flights of stairs the very morning of my flights! When I left New Zealand for Russia, I trusted God for divine strength and help.

Psalm 56:3-4 (ESV) says when we are afraid, we will trust the Lord. We trust God as an act of the will, not because we are fearful, but as an act of praise to God. A man tried to attack me with a knife in the train in Russia, but we stood on the faithfulness and protection of God for safety.

Psalm 107:20 (ESV) tells us we are to speak the word, and God will send his word.

In the prayer room at the Palma Soriano Church, in distress, the man shared his wife lay unconscious, dying in hospital. Even though only fifty-five pounds, after prayer, she recovered! God sent his angels to the hospital. As foreigners, we could not visit her in hospital. We laid hands on this broken man. God touched him, after we prayed, that God would send his word to the hospital and heal his wife. Three weeks later, a tiny lady testified in church that she had been unconscious. Though every day she heard the doctors say she will die today, every day, from the moment we prayed, she felt better and better. She recovered consciousness after and is alive and well today!

THE MAN AND HIS WIFE AND FAMILY
AFTER JESUS HEALED HER

These are just some verses in Psalms that have blessed me and changed my life.

Change gear and allow these verses to transform your life. Gain confidence in the gear of faith through reading and declaring the word of God. Read faith-filled books. Feed your mind on miracles, read the books of those who moved in miracles, and have no doubt God will do it for you. Recognise you are moving forward in an unfamiliar vehicle, that you need to learn an alternative way of operation!

Psalm 119:89-93 ESV, the Word of God is the foundation of our faith. God's Word will stand forever. "Your Word O Lord is eternal."

> Jesus says, "Man cannot live by bread alone but by every word that comes from the mouth of God."
> (—Matthew 4:4 ESV)

The word is the food and foundation of faith. The word of God can create a resistless faith, never daunted, that never gives up or fails.

> In the beginning was the word, and the word was with God, and the word was God.
> (—John 1:1 ESV)

As Jesus is the word, we base our faith on Jesus Christ.

> The word became flesh and dwelt among us.
> (—John 1:14 ESV)

That is Jesus, the anointed one, the Son of the Living God. Just as the Father manifested in Jesus, the Father is in us. The Father did the works through Jesus and does the works through us today.

Knowledge of the word reveals Jesus and brings faith. Without simple knowledge of the word, it limits our faith. There is a rest of faith we enter into. This rest causes us to cease from our own works, from our own struggles, and from making our own plans (Hebrews 4:1-13 ESV). We focus on God's plan and yield to that plan. Even though I had no desire to visit Uganda, when I had three dreams where I visited Uganda with an old friend, I yielded to the plan, resting in his purpose.

UGANDA

UGANDA

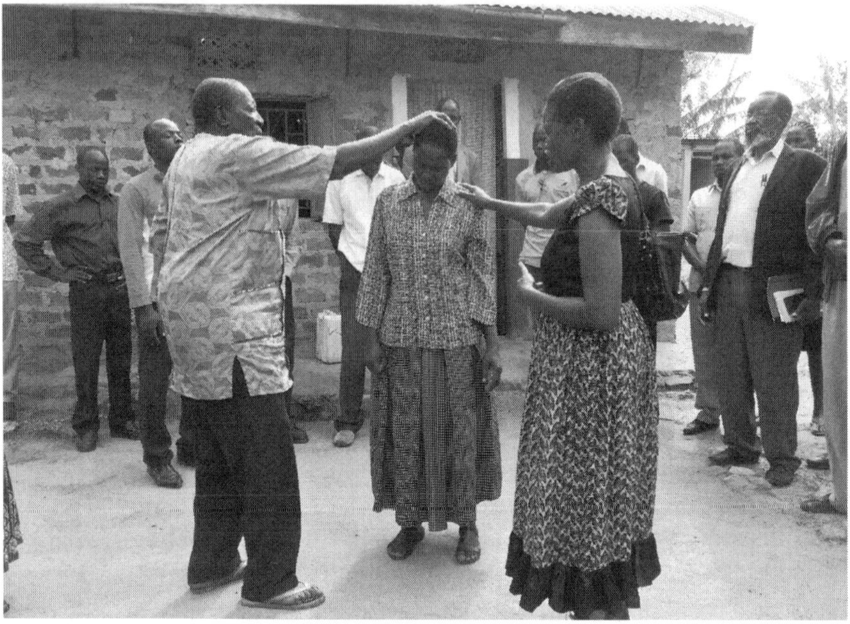

UGANDA BISHOP AND BEA

John 6:28-29 (ESV) tell us we believe on him whom God the Father sent, and we rest. The Father does the works through us; there is no struggle or striving.

Matthew 7:7-8 (ESV), "Everyone who asks receives," we ask and then we receive. God says, "We do not have because we do not ask" (James 4:2 ESV). When I did not ask, I did not receive! I asked God for signs and wonders, and God did it. At the Bhutan border, Jesus visited ten children. They spoke of seeing the devil and shared their experiences in heaven. In Darjeeling, gold dust came on the worship leader's head. I asked for glory to come, and people received flowers in heaven, experienced Jesus coming to them, and had amazing experiences. I felt nothing, I declared Jesus is here, and he walked in the meetings. People looked upon him.

Faith-filled words overrule and free us from the law of sin and death and its forces, ruled by Satan since the fall of Adam. We live through faith in Jesus Christ, the Son of God, and under the law of the spirit of life (Romans 1:4, 8:2 ESV).

THE WORD + FAITH = FAITH-FILLED WORDS

When we know his power, his Holy Spirit in us manifests his works. When we are filled with the Holy Spirit, we know our identity. I am in Christ. He is in God and in the Holy Spirit, dwelling in us. He who dwells in God does the works because God's law sets us free (Ephesians 5:18, Romans 8:2 ESV). Because we have our inheritance from God, the law of sin and death cannot touch us. We are free to do the works of God. We are to speak the words of God. When we speak faith-filled words, we open the door and God gives us more faith.

Romans 10:17 (ESV) says faith comes by hearing the message, and the message is heard through the word of Christ. Faith here is active, not passive. We must speak and do it. Remember, God spoke, and it happened. Christianity is called the great confession.

In a big church in Cuba, we spoke healing, and healings happened in the hospitals. In India, we spoke over pieces of paper—prayer requests—and God healed a crippled child.

I prayed for a pastor at the back of a church where I minister in Cuba. He had a prostate problem. A year later, I shared a meal with a pastor's family in another area. A young woman I did not know was there at the table. She said, "You prayed for my father last year, and it healed him."

I said, "That is wonderful. Who and where was that?"

She then told me about him, and I remembered the occasion.

She said, "You told him, if the symptoms return, he must speak the word of God over his body and rebuke the devil, tell him to get away with his deceit and lies, proclaim healing. A few months went by, and the symptoms returned. He remembered what you said and told them to go. He has never had another problem. Today Jesus healed him."

We must stand on the word of God; mental assent is no good. Power and authority must come from agreement with God. If we don't agree, there will be no power. We don't depend on what we see and what we sense. If we did, we would do nothing.

Though I saw and sensed feeling nothing, I prayed for a woman in. If I waited for the feeling to come, I would pray for nobody! We stand on the word and move in by faith (Hebrews 11:11 ESV). We have the total confident expectation as it depends on the facts. These are the facts we look with the eyes of faith; we depend on the word. We stand, we move in, and we do what God has for us to do.

Romans 10:9-10 (ESV) says it is what we say! We are to confess and declare the word of God, as confession is made unto salvation. What we say is our faith speaking. Committed, for years, I quietly read the word of God. When I realised what this scripture meant, my life changed. I used to think when I heard the word of God from some anointed preacher or from the pulpit, that God spoke, and I heard, and faith would come. God showed me this had only a degree of truth. Once he showed me I needed to speak the word of God when I read the word, then I heard the word, and faith came. As I did this, my faith grew, and my life changed. I read and confessed the word. I wrote the verses that seemed good to me.

Every Saturday morning I would take time to go over all the verses written that week, highlighting and confessing them. As I did this week by week, God spoke to me through them, I knew them, and the word of God became living and active in my life.

> The word is near you: it is in your mouth and in your heart, that is the word of faith we are proclaiming. (—Romans 10:8 ESV)

The word must be in our mouths. We must proclaim the word of faith. What we confess controls us.

(Proverbs 6:2 ESV), we are not to be trapped by our words. For we are to be careful how we think as our thoughts shape our life. (Proverbs 4:20-24). Only say what God says and agree with God by faith.

> Do two walk together except they are agreed to do so.
> (—Amos 3:3 ESV)

Many people think this verse is speaking about marriage, but that is again only part of it. How can we walk with God if we are not agreeing with his word? We can have whatever we say. The words of our mouth are not to bind us. This is not positive thinking, mind over matter. We are to run towards the enemy and speak faith-filled words. David did this with Goliath.

> I come against you in the name of the Lord Almighty, the God of the armies of Israel whom you have defied. This day the Lord will hand you over to me, and I will strike you and cut off your head.
> (—1 Samuel 17:45-48 ESV)

To be afraid to act or speak before we notice the manifestation is to doubt God's word.

We are to confess Jesus is Lord over all (Philippians 2:9-11 ESV). Jesus is Lord over Satan through us, as we confess him, his word, his name, and resist Satan in Jesus's name and through the power of the blood (Revelation 12:10-11 ESV).

> The Lord is my shepherd, I shall not want.
> (—Psalm 23:1 ESV)

He is Jehovah Jireh, my provider. He provided all my needs and even my wants.

When we left NZ with $800 and no job and travelled the world for more than twenty years unpaid, we had divine provision.

In North India, a young woman prayed, "Lord, I want to ride an elephant!" Now going where we go, what a difficult prayer. But nothing is impossible to God. He even gives us our wants! In the early morning, driving to the meeting in the far west of Nepal, along came a decorated elephant. There on the road, the mahout drove it! We raced the car to stop the driver, and all piled out! Great consternation, many laughs and thrills for Ada, as we watched the experience never before experienced. What happened could not be imagined. We had no way for Ada to mount the beast! Usually, there is a platform but not in a remote road in Nepal! So what could we do? After the driver got the animal to kneel, she, a larger lady, climbed up the back of the animal. What a sight, and how we laughed and laughed as she spread-eagled across the back of the elephant, pulling herself up! But Ada enjoyed every minute of her ride on the elaborately-decorated animal, and we collected her further along the road after God answered her prayer, though not what she needed, and gave her what she wanted. Isn't that just our God in his love, he gave her heart's desire.

Mia prayed, "Lord, I want to visit a really nice house. There must be some nice houses in this wilderness of poverty." Everywhere in North India, we had only seen very poor areas. Going to a meeting, we stopped outside an enormous house with a gatehouse.

"Here we are," the leader said.

At the gate house outside the enormous wall, the man opened the gate, and we went in through the grounds to the front door. The guard opened it, and all ten of us filed in. We all followed, looking to the right at a beautiful shining stainless steel kitchen, like one Mia said she had never seen. Gazing at all, we filed past the sumptuous lounge with the most beautiful swagged red velvet drapes hanging at enormous windows and the ornate furniture. In single file, all ten of us marched silently up the enormous staircase with ornate carved sides to the amazing balcony. When we reached the landing, we looked up, and our gaze reached a huge painting on the wall—a painting of Krishna.

Our leader said, "Let's get out quick!"

What consternation, realising we were in the wrong place, we all turned like clockwork and filed out. We walked back down the stairwell, past the kitchen, past the beautiful lounge, out the front door across the path past the guard house and filed back into the car. In the car, we laughed and laughed! We had walked right through somebody's house there in North India, and nobody had stopped us. The guard man had let us in, all in answer to my sister's prayer. Isn't God amazing? He gives us not just what we want, not just what we need, but also the cry of a heart!

FAY AND MIA

Isaiah 53:3-5, I am free from every sin, sickness, disease, sorrow, and grief.

What grief with the alienation of my entire extended family, after my mother and stepfather both died within three weeks of each other. I thought my heart would break, but God, in his love, reconciled the situation, and within six months, relationships restored. We are free as his love fills our lives.

We must refuse to bow our confession to death's laws, the same as Shadrach, Meshach, and Abednigo refused to bow down to the idol (Daniel 3:17, 25, 27 ESV). If we compromise to keep something, we will lose it.

HOW TO HAVE SOME KEYS TO FAITH

There are four things for faith: agreement with God's word, the word is God's will. No questions, no ifs. Because we have no doubt with our mind, our head, our heart, we confess with our lips, and we act on the word, the elements obey (Romans 10:17 ESV).

We believed God when we arrived in Miami with only two connections! There were no questions, just implicit agreement with God's word. We trusted his ability to lead, guide, and provide! Our New Zealand departure was huge, out of neutral, out of park, and beginning to change gear. As we moved ahead, we learnt and gained confidence, we moved into gear. We had never walked this way before. A new dimension opened up to us in a different vehicle of faith. With no car, no computer, just our bags and $800, no ifs, we confessed God's provision, accepted he would lead, and moved forward by faith. In a Spanish home, with no English, sleeping on stretcher beds, eating beans and rice for this NZ couple, what a challenge! Kevin wanted to know what way north, south, east, and west were and walked exploring the neighbourhood to establish his bearings. A homeless woman who slept in her car began to help us. God provided this special lady to take us to her pastor. She really wanted us to meet her pastor, and as a result, we not only met him, but also his brother, his father, and his whole family. They became part of our lives; the brother, a pastor and dentist, took over our dental care for twenty years. Now he has attended to all our dental needs, a total provision of God. As we trusted God, his father, a doctor, assisted us in the first year in Miami with some specific medical needs. God is so faithful; he looks after us at every turn. As we agreed with God's word, we watched him act. In two weeks in Miami, we received all that we needed through the meetings we did, as doors opened through this woman and others. Everything provided for us to travel to Cuba and be able to bless the believers in Cuba. With only $800, that would not go far, but the Lord God provided, as he has continued to do so for more than twenty years of travel.

HOMELESS LADY AND ROSIE

In another divine appointment, we needed somewhere to stay for a weekend of ministry in the Keys. We met a family who took us in and continued to do so for a long time on every visit to the area. They became our friends. He was a lawyer, and she worked for him as his office manager. Their home, always very private, as not only did they live in a private area, but also they only allowed certain people into their circle of friends. Yet God prepared them as they opened their home to us. They opened their office to us, and when we set up the ministry in the United States, they allowed us to use their address as the address for the ministry. We needed an address for FCM, and we could register the ministry in Florida because of their love and faithfulness. How amazing God is as he gave us the gift of their friendship, the gift of their love.

OUR SOLICITOR FRIENDS

Divine appointments were everywhere. Everywhere we travelled, our friend with the car opened up churches, the brothers opened up churches, and so God began to use us amongst the Spanish in Miami for an amazing time.

Hebrews 4:14 (ESV) says, "Let us hold firmly to the faith we profess," the absolute integrity of the word. We are to know what our rights are and hold fast to our confession, in the face of contrary evidence, to put the word in the place of our senses. Christ is the high priest of our confession. Hebrews 10:23 says, "We are to hold unswervingly with no wavering," and say what God says.

> We walk by faith, not by sight.
> (—2 Corinthians 5:7 ESV)

We don't place confidence in what is visible; we consider it ours until it changes to become visible and we have it.

When we returned from Cuba, one of these brothers greeted us at the airport. He took us to a home and put a handful of money in Kevin's pocket and said, "I'm taking you to Mexico. This will help you survive 'til then." We stayed with a man who became our friend in a foreclosed house, which the bank repossessed, a provision for these travelers by faith in God's plan. When we cling to the faith we profess, God moves in ways far beyond what we could ever ask or think.

A SPECIAL FRIEND WHO HAS BLESSED US AGAIN AND AGAIN

HOW TO HAVE THE MEASURE OF FAITH

Romans 12:3 (ESV) says we have the measure of faith. God gives the same amount to everyone; it's what we do with it that counts. It's not the size of a grain of mustard seed! The measure is the same as God used to raise Jesus from the dead. When God raised Jesus from the dead, that became a far greater act of faith than when he created the world. No principality or power opposed him at creation (Ephesians 1:16-23, 2:1-8 ESV).

We arrived in Iowa in the Ford, which had taken us all over the country for several years. After we drove nine hours from Indiana, we parked it, ready for our visit to the pastor the next morning. When we awoke and were setting off for the appointment, the key turned, but the car failed to respond! What a problem! Our friends organised Kevin would go with Ev to fix the car and Denise would visit the pastor. They left the car at the garage, where they gave an assurance that it may be an electrical fault. A week later, $700 and mounting for assessment, after a trip back to Indiana in our friend's car, the Ford still failed to respond!

Kevin and Ev departed to sort the car! They made a decision to kill the deal! Ev paid the bill, and they proceeded downtown, where they changed the ownership papers from Ev's van to our name, and we left later that week with a vehicle provided by our friends after another divine provision of God as he cared for us. We didn't have to buy another car; God provided through our friends who had agreed that if the car did not mend, they would give us their car! We all have the same measure of faith.

In Acts 3, Peter and John came to the temple and prayed for the cripple. Peter said, "What I have, I give you." He gave away faith. Jesus lived to show God's glory on earth "to bring many sons and daughters to glory" (Hebrews 2:10 ESV). The Living God has chosen you and me to put his power and glory in us, that we would bring many sons and daughters to glory!

Jesus said, "The works that I do, you shall do."
(—John 14:12 ESV)

You and I, by faith, can do greater works than Jesus did.

In an area far east in Cuba, we prayed for a family. The grandfather had cancer, and the daughter could not have children. We are to give away what we have, for that is what Peter and John did at the temple with the crippled man. They gave healing and deliverance to the man. We gave away healing, and when we returned to the church two years later, there were the miracles: twin babies and the grandfather healed of prostate cancer. We did the works of the Father, loved them and prayed for them, and God healed.

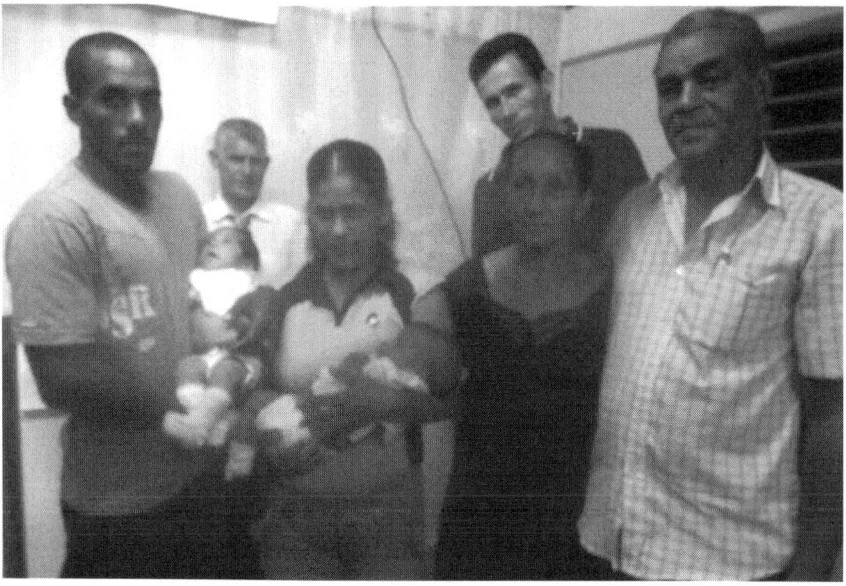

THE GRAND FATHER AND BABIES

When we are born again, we are a new creation; we bring heaven to earth. Seated in heavenly places through faith, by faith, we bring all the elements of heaven to earth. The divine nature of God has come to us; we are a new creation, an heir of Jesus. The nature of Jesus lives in us. Everything of the Father comes to us, to you and to me (Ephesians 2:6; Colossians 3:13; 2 Corinthians 5:17 ESV).

In John 15:16 (ESV), Jesus chose, appointed, and anointed us to go and bring forth fruit.

We are to present all that he is. We are to bear the fruit, then God will answer. The Father lived in Jesus and lives in us (John 14:9-10 ESV).

It says in 2 Peter 1:4 (ESV) that we have received his divine nature, his divine power has given us everything we need, and we are part of his nature. "For we died with Christ." It's an exchange; he took our sin and gave us his life. The old has gone, the new has come. We recognise we live by faith, the faith of God, that Jesus lives in us and his nature is our nature (2 Timothy 2:11 ESV).

> The Lord has done this, and it is marvelous in our eyes.
> (—Matthew 21:42 ESV)

Jesus did significant works because of his knowledge of the Father; he did what he observed the Father did. The Lord has given us the power as Jesus lives in us. We do what we read Jesus did.

We visited in homes, and we met so many people. Amongst them were so many with witchcraft idols on shelves; people suffered, oppressed by the devil. In one home lived a woman who suffered effects of a stroke. There, in that home, we encouraged her. After we prayed, laid hands on her, anointed her with oil, we discussed and explained how to exercise the areas of her body damaged by the stroke. So we showed her how to move her arm and leg; she was to exercise and speak the word of God over her body. A few days later, she appeared at the church. Until then she could not walk any distance, but now she came. She walked to the church that began the healing; that healing came by faith, existed by faith. By faith, she walked to the church; by faith, she moved. She trusted God that God, true to his word, had healed her and he began an amazing work in her.

> I give you power over all the power of the enemy, authority, to trample on snakes.
> (—Luke 10:19 ESV)

We have power from on high to overcome all the power of the enemy because we have the faith of God, the same faith Jesus had is in us; it's what we do with it.

> For everyone born of God overcomes the world. This is the victory that has overcome the world, even our faith.
> (—1 John 5:4 (ESV)

Satan is under our feet; we are victorious (Psalm 8:6, Ephesians 1:22, Hebrews 2:8 ESV).

> We overcome by the blood of the lamb and the word of our testimony, by the word of faith.
> (—Revelation 12:11 ESV)

My brother in Myanmar shared and showed us many pictures of cripples walking, blind people seeing, and the deaf hearing! In an outdoor meeting in Cuba, faith arose in the meeting as a man shouted, touching his ear, "I can hear, I can hear! I suffered deafness in one ear, and now Jesus has healed me!"

There is no limit to the power that God will cause to come upon those who cry to him in faith. We are to pursue and aim for faith, remembering there is a good fight of faith! We are called to fight in a war where we use a shield to protect us and quench and extinguish every attack of the enemy (1 Timothy 5:11-12 ESV).

> In all circumstances take up the shield of faith, with which you can extinguish all the flaming darts of the evil one . . .
> (—Ephesians 6:16 ESV)

The devil cannot get near us when we say, "Now, Lord, look after this property of yours. Lord, I claim your victory over the devil."

> The righteous "shall live by faith."
> (—Galatians 3:11 ESV)

We are not only to live by, but also out of faith. When we are in right standing with God, we are just and righteous. Another translation says, "He who through and by faith is declared righteous and in right standing with God will live." Just as God credited Abraham's faith to him as righteousness, when we place our confidence in God, he credits our faith to us as righteousness (Galatians 3:6 ESV).

> And be found in Him, not having mine own righteousness, that comes from the law, but that which is through faith in Christ, the righteousness that comes from God and is faith.
> (—Philippians 3:9 KJV)

If you get to know God's righteousness, if you get to know the faith of righteousness, you can dare to stand and face anything in the world.

Romans 14:23 (ESV) says everything that does not come from faith is sin. Faith is trust, where we come into a place that is immoveable.

DOES GOD HEAR YOUR FAITH?

> Did you receive the Spirit by observing the law or by believing what you heard, or the hearing of your faith . . . Does God give you the Spirit to work miracles because you observe the law or because you believe what you heard? Or by faith?
> (—Galatians 3:2, 5 ESV)

God listened to Abraham's faith and credited it to him as righteousness. We are children of Abraham. Does God listen to have no doubt of your faith? Is he moving through you to bring healing and deliverance?

The Greek says in the hearing of your faith, God must catch our faith's cry. In Mark 5, it speaks of a woman, an outcast, who bled for twelve years. Though despised, God listened to her faith! She had lost everything; she wanted to be whole. The virtue of Jesus flowed to her.

Jesus said, "Who touched me?"

"Me," she said, as she had to confess it.

She was not just healed, but also made whole. When we feel the touch of Jesus, it makes us whole. As we said earlier, faith is a choice. We choose to have no doubt that the word of God is true and act upon it. Her faith cried out to Jesus.

Each trip to minister overseas, I spoke the word of God over my life. I will lay hands on the sick. I will see the demons flee (Mark 16:15-18, Matthew 28:16-20, Acts 1:8 ESV). In 1994, I spoke I will pray and cripple will walk. That year in Cuba, we pulled a crippled man out of his wheelchair! A young man of twenty-eight years was crying out to God, "Lord, I want to walk. Lord, I want to walk!" One helper listened to his cry and moved to assist him. Because of ministry, this man walked for the first time in his life! God must hear our faith. Since then, many crippled people have walked. All praise and thanks to God who sets the captives free.

THE MAN WALKING

Faith requires practise to grow. As we use our faith, faith comes and grows. Faith requires practise to be strong, and it comes from God's word released through acts of obedience. Faith requires single-mindedness, for God has to stretch our faith to make us grow.

EXAMPLES OF FAITH

Hebrews 11 is a marvelous chapter about the heroes of faith. Any discussion about faith must linger and look at the triumphs of some spiritual giants. Though we have already looked at the faith of Abraham, the friend of God, there are many others. When you recognise God has brought you to the place of faith, let it be that your faith is for the glory of God.

Enoch agreed and walked with God. He moved in the divine direction. With mutual trust, he kept in step with God.

Noah, a remarkable man, walked with God. Known as a righteous man, perfect in his generation, Noah moved with Godly fear by faith. He spent 120 years building a huge boat in an area far from water, and the people mocked and ridiculed him, for he did something he had no reason for doing it, except that God had commanded him to do it. Genuine faith built the ark, but genuine faith did not shut the door.

These are only two of all the men in the Bible history who walked with God. Enoch and Noah did not run ahead of God; they never lagged behind him.

Amran and Jochebed saved and hid Moses by faith. This faith inspired hope, created courage, and caused rational actions, and cooperated with the purposes of God. By faith, Moses, when older, refused to be known as the son of the pharaoh's daughter—he identified with the Israelites. By faith, he left Egypt and lived to trust God. Faith makes possible the activity of God. The Israelites had to obey to take Jericho. This became the obedience of faith, as faith by obedience prepares the way for the activities of God. God's commands seem to be almost impossible, beyond our reason, but are intended to fling us back upon himself.

Caleb knew that they would enter the land God gave them. He had faith when faced with a forty-year delay! (Numbers 13:30, 14:6-9 ESV).

In Luke 1:37-38 (ESV), when the angel came to Mary, she said, "Nothing is impossible to God." She believed God and trusted him for her own and the baby's future, and she worshipped him. Because of her faith, as God observed her righteous life, she found favor with God. She said, "How can this be?" By faith, she accepted what the angel said and risked everything. Faith must have its actions completed in obedience, or disaster will follow.

Faith works by love, our love for God, our obedience to his voice and his word. Jesus said, "If you love me, you will obey what I command" (John 14:15 ESV). Faith depends on our surrender.

> And if I have the gift of prophecy and can fathom all mysteries and all knowledge; and if I have a faith that can move mountains but have not love I am nothing.
> (—1 Corinthians 13:2 ESV)

We need to pray, "Lord, I want to be a channel of your love. Fill me with your love." When we do this, wonderful things will happen.

In Vietnam, I hugged a tiny woman who came for prayer. I prayed in English, she understood it in Vietnamese, and the words she heard were "Forgive, forgive!" I did not ever say "Forgive, forgive!" I just prayed. She had decided that day she would never forgive her husband again! As he was an alcoholic, with the associated behaviors, she became angry. Healed and delivered, her marriage restored and healed that day! God poured his love into her life. And from the moment we hugged, they were free, healed. Praise the name of Jesus. We are to have faith in God and power with God through the knowledge of God's word. That night the pastors came to visit us and said, "We got a miracle today!" When we asked what miracle, they replied, "We are excited as when you prayed today for our parents. God healed and restored their marriage."

When we change gear and move into faith, the faith of God, we recognise that if we stall or miss the gear or pause in the journey because we lose our focus, we can slow down or move into reverse, which causes many hindrances to faith. The lack of understanding that we are a new creation stops and hinders our ability to recognise who we are and hinders our ability to act. Faith acts (Colossians 1:22; 1 Peter 1:23, 2:9; Revelation 1:5-6; Hebrews 2:9-14 ESV).

The lack of understanding of our place in him and his place in us robs us of our true identity in Christ. "In Christ–In Him" appears 134 times in the New Testament. We are in him and he is in us (Colossians 3:11, Ephesians 3:6 ESV).

The lack of understanding of righteousness keeps people in bondage, as many of us have an inadequate idea of what righteousness is and what it gives (James 5:16; 1 John 1:9).

There is a lack of understanding of our privilege and right to use the name of Jesus. In reality, there is brief mention of the power of the blood and name of Jesus in the body of Christ today (Mark 16:17-18, John 14:12-14, John 16:23-24 ESV).

There is lack of understanding about acting on the word. Counterattack defeats more people than anything else, as believing demands our action (James 1:22, John 3:21, Luke 8:21, Proverbs 3:5 ESV).

There is lack of understanding that we are to hold fast to our confession of faith. Our faith is to keep pace with our confession (Hebrews 4:14 ESV).

There is lack of forgiveness of others. We must forgive and not hold anything against anyone (Mark 11:25-26; Galatians 5:6; 1 Corinthians 13:1-3 ESV). Love is the power charge behind the God kind of faith.

That is what our little lady did; she forgave, and she brought freedom, deliverance, which released God's power to love.

HOW TO DEVELOP THIS FAITH?

There are some ways we can do this: Receive Jesus as the developer of our faith. Put our faith on the line and allow the word to be first in our lives. We should fill our lives with the word through reading and meditation on the word. When we act on the word and change our confession, this changes the atmosphere, for confession brings possession. Live a life of love. When we confess what God has provided in Christ Jesus and recognise what is ours in the new birth, faith arises. What we are to the Father, what Jesus is doing for us now, and what God can do through us become a living revelation in our lives (Hebrews 7:25 ESV).

Do we have faith or fear, belief or unbelief? To have fear is to move, to pause, to stop, or even to consider moving into reverse. It means we no longer move forward in faith, but we pause to change gear and listen to our doubts, to our rational minds, to our logic and reason. Fear is to have a broad range of emotions that embrace both the secular and the religious worlds. Secular fear is the natural sensing of alarm caused by the expectation of imminent danger, pain, or disaster. Religious fear appears as the result of awe and reverence toward a supreme power (*Holman Bible Dictionary*).

Fear is a spiritual force, Satan's destructive power, the substance of things not desired (Matthew 14:30 ESV).

Fear is defined by *Strong's Concordance* as "fright; to frighten; to make afraid; fearing; to put or to be in fear; fearfulness; A fearful thing or deed; great fear; fearfully; terrible terror; terrors; to make shake; horror; dread; dreadful; to be formidable; to be startled by a sudden alarm; stand in awe; to revere; reverence; fear of God. a feeling of distress and apprehension or alarm caused by impending danger, pain, etc."

How often have we felt one of these? If we are truthful, most of us will say often! The sin of fear is unbelief (Isaiah 51:12-13 ESV). We are told not to fear 365 times in the Bible, one for each day of the year. It must be an enormous problem for us if God speaks about it so many times.

In Isaiah 41:10–14, the words "fear not" appear three times. It gives the reasons we are not to fear; for example, in verse 10, it says God is with us. There is no need for dismay as he will strengthen us. He undertakes responsibility for us as he gives us his actual strength. While we have the use of his name, he gives himself to us as he is our God. We have his companionship all the time and are safe in his hands. Worry is a sin, a lack of trust, for no one can worry and trust at the same time. We are to trust and obey.

> Isaiah 43:1-7 (ESV) gives us reason not to fear: But now thus says the LORD, he who created you, O Jacob, he who formed you, O Israel: "Fear not, for I have redeemed you; I have called you by name, you are mine. When you pass through the waters, I will be with you; and through the rivers, they shall not overwhelm you; when you walk through fire you shall not be burnt, and the flame shall not consume you. For I am the LORD your God, the Holy One of Israel, your Savior. I give Egypt as your ransom, Cush and Seba in exchange for you. Because you are precious in my eyes, and honoured, and I love you, I give men in return for you, peoples in exchange for your life. Fear not, for I am with you; I will bring your offspring from the east, and from the west I will gather you. I will say to the north, Give up, and to the south, Do not withhold; bring my sons from afar and my daughters from the end of the earth, everyone who is called by my name, whom I created for my glory, whom I formed and made."

He promises to go with us through the waters and the fires. They will not overwhelm us, and he will not fail us, for he loves us. Nothing works against his will. In verse 4, he promises to give us spiritual fruit. We are to forget the former things. Seed planted will appear to fail, but we will rejoice at the fruit.

We are not to remember the former things, past things, as when we do, we give them power over us. When the devil comes to remind us of the past, we are to remind him of his future (Isaiah 43:18 ESV).

In Isaiah 44:1-5, God says fear not, for he will pour out joy. We are not to be afraid because God is the God of abundant blessings, comfort, and joy, which he promises to pour out on us. In verse 3, it says he will pour water on the thirsty ground on him who is thirsty. Are you thirsty today?

When I preached for the first time, it was in Cuba. The year before, I had prayed fervently, "Lord, send joy." Everyone, including me, wept and wept. Only two people laughed, I remember them. A year later, I visited again and had not even prayed about the joy. God poured out the river wherever we travelled. The people were dry and thirsty. Do you want more today? God later released his joy on those believers in Cuba and will do so on you when you yield to him. God promises great spiritual blessings. God's heart is to bless us and to give us gifts. He wants to give us gladness. The Holy Spirit is the best antidote for fear. When he comes, fear becomes thanksgiving and rejoicing. He brings restoration.

> Who are you that you fear mortal men, the sons of men who are but grass, that you forget the Lord your maker? And fear continually every day and live I and constant terror.
> (—Isaiah 51:12-13 ESV)

Fear of the oppressor is foolishness.

Unbelief leads us to forget God, makes us become people-conscious, problem-conscious. Unbelief causes us to take our eyes off God and look at the circumstances. As unbelief is insidious, we don't even realise we have it! We do not have to worry and waste our lives, for worry is sin. God says he comforts us. Fear of man brings a snare.

Isaiah 54:1-17 (ESV) has four reasons not to fear. Basically, here, the Lord says fear not as he is our husband; he loves us, cherishes us; and nothing can overtake or hurt us as he is with us to protect and deliver and care for us. We are not to allow shame or disgrace to confound us as we have his righteousness and live under grace, not law. The law ceased when Jesus died and rose again. Fear is under the curse of the law (Deuteronomy 28:65-67 ESV). God is for us and loves us and will never abandon us (1 Corinthians 1:30 ESV). We receive the gift of righteousness. God has such a great love for us. He wants us to forget there ever was sin between his heart and ours. So we cannot imagine him failing or forgetting us (Romans 5:17 ESV). The remedy for fear is faith and love.

1 John 4:16-18 (ESV) says, "Perfect love casts out fear." Love is made perfect because we dwell in him who is love. Fear is dangerous, as it turns into fact the things we fear. Fear creates evil just as faith creates good. While fear connects us to Satan and puts us in line with destruction, faith connects us with the Holy Spirit and the anointing. The devil's fears are always lies. His suggestions are always lies, and they cannot harm. If fear comes from Satan, then we must conclude there is nothing to fear. Fear is my confidence in sickness, snakes, natural problems, and it works the same as faith.

Did we fear when driving in Nepal and men with fiery torches banged on the van doors shouting, "If you're on the road tomorrow, we will kill you and burn the van!"? Did we fear when we drove out of Nepal in the strike with no cars on the road? Did we fear when they were burning buildings in Bangkok and there was razor wire and men with guns in the street where we stayed? Did we fear when we went to have dinner with our pastor friend in Yangon and two bombs had just exploded in the road? Did we fear when we were summoned to immigration in Vietnam and we didn't go?

Absolutely not! We are a people of faith, not fear!

HIMALAYAN RANGE

NEPAL CONFERENCE

HIMALAYAN TEAM

While fear works or comes by hearing the word of the world, fear is now! Satan tries to take what God gives. Jesus gave Peter power, and Satan took it from him by the actions of the wind and the waves. What we gaze at and what we sense affects what we confess. Peter lost the power by doubting he could walk on water! (Matthew 14:30 ESV) Fear develops through meditating and acting on Satan's lies. Fear demands compromise, as Satan supports and actively develops fear. When acted upon, fear becomes doubt and unbelief. Fear is not natural to the born-again believer and has to be received before it can enter the heart and stop faith (1 John 4:15-18 ESV).

We receive what we continually look at, as if we look at the difficulties they overcome us (Proverbs 4:20-25, Matthew 14:30 ESV). Fear acted on produces the law of sin and death, whereas faith acted on produces the law of the spirit of life. To stop fear before it enters is an act of the will. We don't accept the thoughts (Psalm 118:6; 2 Corinthians 10:3-5 ESV).

God has not given us fear; we choose it (Romans 8:15; Galatians 5:22-24; 2 Timothy 1:7 ESV). Jesus delivered us from fear.

Fear brings failure, torment, guilt, condemnation, sickness, and death, and these allow Satan to control us. As fear disconnects you from the supernatural, it binds you to the natural. Since fear brings feelings, feelings control us; fear has no authority until we accept it. We must confront fear in the power of the Holy Spirit. God is looking for people who *fear not.*

Faith brings forth knowledge, fellowship, and communion. If we see imperfect faith, full of doubt, a wavering condition, it always comes of imperfect knowledge (Wigglesworth).

Wigglesworth said all lack of faith is because of not feeding on the word. You need it every day. How can you enter a life of faith? Feed on the Living Christ of whom this word is full. As you get taken up with the glorious fact and the wondrous presence of the Living Christ, the faith of God will spring up within you.

Vine's defines *doubt* as "to stand in two ways, implying uncertainty which way to take, said of believers whose faith is small; being anxious through a distracted state of mind; of wavering between hope and fear."

The law of doubt will produce death (Romans 6:23 ESV).

Job 3:25 (ESV) tells us the thing we fear and are afraid of will come upon us.

Romans 8:6 (ESV) says the mind of the flesh (which is sense and reason without the Holy Spirit) is *death.* Death comprises all the miseries arising from sin.

Romans 14:23 says acting on doubt brings condemnation from God. If there is no conviction of the approval of God, the action is sinful. Whatever does not originate from faith is sin. Faith refuses to consider a reason to doubt. We struggle when we are uncertain of something!

They always render *unbelief* as disobedience in the Revised Bible version. This means believe not, disbelieve, to be unbelieving, unbeliever, faithlessness, unfaithfulness, without faith, willfully, perversely disobedient, to obey not (Strong's). They define unbelief in Vine's as want of faith, without faith, did not believe.

The greatest weakness in the world is unbelief. It says in 1 John 5:5 (ESV), we overcome the world through belief that Jesus is the Son of God. This belief causes adherence, trust, and reliance on the word of God. Unbelief causes us to stagger, robs us of our inheritance, and causes us to waver. Wavering arise from distrust of God's divine power.

James 1:6-7 (ESV) says, "He who wavers let him not think he will receive anything from the Lord."

Passive wavering gets us nothing. The one who wavers, hesitates, doubts, is like the billowing surge out at sea that is blown hither and thither and tossed by the wind. Wavering arise from distrust of God's divine power as unbelief robs us of the blessings of God.

What prevents us from belief? Our rational thinking shaped by our cultural expectations.

These create insensitivity to the Holy Spirit. It is the way we perceive and sense things. Then our expectations control it and cause our actions. Faith-filled words overthrow and pull down unbelief.

For years, I read the word of God. Unbelief choked my life. Unable to live without doubt, I found it difficult to understand that God could do things for me. I watched him do many things, and he answered prayer, but when people prayed for me, I would sense nothing. People who ministered to me would say, "I glimpse that wonderful things will happen for you, God is really touching you." But I would sense nothing! I didn't realise it was unbelief. One day I read in Hebrews 3:19 (ESV) that the Israelites could not enter into the promised land because of their unbelief. Their unbelief shut them out. We too cannot enter the land of God's promises because of our unbelief. Many times we don't even realise that this is what it is. Can you identify with this? It was difficult to accept God could do things for me. I read on into Hebrews 4, where it says, in verse 2, that the message the Israelites heard was of no benefit to them because they did not combine it with faith.

The light turned on for me. I realised that, for years, I had read the Bible but never combined it with faith! I had never leaned my entire personality on God in absolute trust and confidence in his power. The day I read this, I realised that the unbelief that had been present in my life had finished. Sometime before, I had started to read the word of God aloud and proclaim it over my life. After God spoke to me at the close of 1989, calling me to the four corners of the earth, I declared every day, by faith, I will go to the nations in the name of Jesus, I will lay hands on the sick, captives will be set free, etc. On those first trips overseas, my faith had arisen as God did amazing things and through me, an ordinary woman!

Unbelief robs us of our inheritance in God. We stand by faith; we fall by unbelief. There is a grave danger of our having two confessions: one would be the integrity of the word, and the other would be of our doubts and fears. Every time we confess weakness and failure, doubt and fear, we go to the level of them. We may pray ardently and earnestly and declare in our prayers our faith in the word, and yet the confession of our mouth will rob us.

We soak ourselves in the word, and gradually, the new image comes forth in our lives. Mental assent, confession without action, is of no use. It is of the senses. We must combine the word with faith, then the confession of the word will bring possession. We base victory on what God says and doing what God says. If the way we act is not by faith, it is by doubt and fear or something else. Many people talk the talk, but few walk the walk! Faith makes us victorious. Faith is the victor.

Jesus is the author and finisher of faith (Hebrews 12:3 ESV).

HOW TO CHANGE GEAR

HOW TO GO WITH A GREEN LIGHT, MOVE INTO OBEDIENCE

MOVE ON

Faith brings obedience; faith and obedience bring relationship.

Someone is waiting on the other side of our obedience! We never know who it could be or what God will do because we obey!

In Myanmar we climbed into green slime to baptise two young men. It was ghastly! Sharen turned to Perry and said, "Would you like to be baptised?"

"Not likely!" he replied.

Perry loved drama and enjoyed playing the Bible characters. He didn't much cope with the teaching but was a tremendous asset in the ministry. Coming from a conservative educated background, he loved coming to these nations, where we were hiding from the police and doing almost illegal things! When we arrived at the conference venue at 6:00 a.m., to be there before the policeman who waited in the street outside watching our building, it did not faze him. And when we stayed 'til 5:00 p.m., to be sure the policeman left before us, all part of the drama, he loved every minute of every drama! He loved it! Over dinner in our Vietnam hotel, Perry asked me, "Will you baptise me? I haven't been baptised."

I hesitated before replying. The difficulties seemed insurmountable! Why Vietnam? Why now? Where could we do it? We were in the middle of a huge city in a hotel with a busy programme! How could we do this? Perry, a great guy who loved adventure, travelled with Sharen, his wife, several times to Myanmar and now to Vietnam. After deliberation, I said, "Why not do it in New Zealand? Then you can have friends, family around you."

"No, no," said Perry, "I want to do it here!"

Again, I pondered the issues. Where could we do it? As we were in a restricted nation, it had to be in secret so we could not attract attention to ourselves in any way! Finally, we decided we would do it in the bath in our bedroom. Just one problem with a smallish bath: How would Perry fit? He's long, thin, and tall. Anyway, with care and attention and perseverance, we organised it all, and I baptised Perry in water, in obedience to the command of the Lord, following the example of Jesus. Perry changed gear that day when he was baptised in obedience as a new believer, deciding to make a statement of his decision to follow Jesus.

Perry, on the other side of my obedience, received his heart's desire—baptism in Vietnam. Because I obeyed God and travelled to Vietnam, there, at the right time for God's purpose for Perry's life, I saw him change gears in his life.

PERRY

VIETNAM MINISTRY

On the second trip to Cuba, I spoke on the blessings and curses at a very difficult meeting in the far east of the island. I will never forget the meeting as it was in the dark because of the power cuts, and as I preached with a tiny torch, a man in the congregation was taking photos with a very high-powered flash, blinding me. This the first night in a new area was difficult. When the altar call came, as we build relationship during the preaching, the people could not see me, just a voice, like on the radio! My memories of the night were of many difficulties. Several years later in this area, the new interpreter said to me, "When you came here three years ago, my life changed! Delivered and set free from the effects of curses, God healed a stomach condition when you prayed for me. I had only been a believer for a short time, and it transformed my family. Because of the change in my life, shortly afterwards, my husband found Jesus as Savior." She is a woman of faith who moved with her husband in deliverance and healing. All this happened because of obedience. She was on the other side of my obedience.

Obedience is to listen to God's word and act accordingly. The translated word "obey" in the Old Testament means "to hear" and is often so translated. In the New Testament, several words describe obedience. One definition is "to hear or to listen in a state of submission." Another New Testament translation means "to trust" or "to persuade, to win over" (*Holman Bible Dictionary*). Vine's says to listen, to attend, to submit, to obey.

"Faith is of the heart—invisible to men. Obedience is conduct and may be observed" (Vine's Expository Dictionary).

Obedience is the response of faith to any instruction from God. Jesus taught that true faith will always be manifested in obedience to God's revealed will. Successful Christian living results from seeking and knowing God's will and then doing it, acting in faith. Obedience to the word of God brings about the work of God. Slow obedience is not obedience. We are to daily obey the voice of God. God wants us to obey, even if we look foolish. We don't know what God will do when we obey. We are to obey and leave the results with God. To obey does not come naturally. The evidence of faith is in obedience.

> Jesus said, "My sheep hear My voice and I know them and they follow Me."
> (—John 10:27 ESV)

We must listen carefully to God's voice. If we are not hearing his voice, maybe we are not obeying.

John G. Lake tells the story of a preacher on the frontier of America. He preached and taught the word across the frontier, teaching strongly against alcohol, smoking, and dance. Often he had to stay in the room above the saloon of the local bar. One day he was waiting in the crowded saloon for his room to be ready. As he looked around him at people dancing, smoking, and drinking, the Holy Spirit spoke. "Get up and dance!" He sat dumbfounded. It couldn't be the voice of God, could it? Three times, the Holy Spirit spoke, and he sat tightly, not daring to move, arguing within himself. Hadn't he preached against all these things? How could God be asking him to dance? After all, he couldn't even dance! Finally, he yielded to the voice of God. He got up and walked across the room to a young woman and said to her, "Will you dance with me?" She nodded her assent and rose to stand beside him. He said to her, "Excuse me a minute, but before I do anything, I always pray." He fell to his knees in the crowded saloon and prayed desperately, praying and praying and praying! Every eye focused on him! As he prayed, he noticed all had gone quiet, then thud! Thud! Thud! Thud! Thud! Thud! He listened carefully, thud, thud . . . Finally, with no more thuds, he opened his eyes and stood to his feet, the only person standing! All the other people were on the floor under the power of the Holy Spirit. He preached the word, and they all came to Jesus. He became a fool for Jesus to obey the voice of God. Those people were on the other side of his obedience!

> Loving me empowers you to obey my commands.
> (—John 14:15 TPT)

If we love Jesus, he empowers us to do what he says. He does not abandon us; he helps us.

John 14:15,21, Jesus said [ESV], "If you love Me you will do what I say." Whatever it speaks about in the Bible, we must do. There are many blessings for us if we obey. We need not ask God for more direction. We just need to do it.

> "Those who truly love me are those who obey my commands. Whoever passionately loves me will be passionately loved by my Father. And I will passionately love you in return and will manifest my life within you." Jesus replied, "Loving me empowers you to obey my word. And my Father will love you so deeply that we will come to you and make you our dwelling place."
> (—John 14:21 TPT)

If we don't love him, we won't do it. The mark of our love for Jesus is our obedience as when we keep his commands, we walk in his love.

For many years, I visited Cuba and wore lipstick, a simple necklace, and earrings. The year before, I had asked the interpreter if I should take these off as women members in the church where I ministered did not wear jewellery or makeup. She had said, "No, you are a western woman, it's okay for you. You are a visitor."

On the way to a meeting in a difficult area, the Lord spoke to me. "Take off your jewellery, you don't need it anymore. Let the beauty of Jesus be seen in you."

From that day, for two years, I did not wear jewellery or makeup in that nation or anywhere. This act brought tremendous acceptance and bonding with the leadership and believers as I identified in this way. But most of all, it brought increased relationship with the Lord. God wants our obedience. I found out later that these items had been offensive to the leadership, but they had never once mentioned it. Later they changed all that, and freedom came for ladies to wear jewellery and makeup.

If we love him, we do what he says as he empowers us to do so!

DENISE AND SONIA IN CUBA

There are blessings promised for obedience.

The supermarket trolleys have a place in the car park to which they should be returned. When I read in a magazine that God had spoken to a woman to return the trolley she used, I had always left my trolley anywhere in the car park near where I had parked my car. When I read this story, I felt the Holy Spirit stir me to put the trolley back. I began to put the trolley back in its correct place. This might sound trivial, but if we really want more of the presence of God in our lives, we will do whatever God tells us to do. God wants wholehearted obedience. Yesterday's obedience is no good for today.

How often do we say, God doesn't speak to me? We have to ask ourselves, are we really listening? Are we obeying God? We must listen carefully and carefully obey.

Deuteronomy 28:1-14 (ESV) speaks of the blessings when we fully obey God. In verse 2, it says all these blessings will come upon us and accompany us. God promises his blessing if we obey. In verse 3, you will be blessed in the city and in the country. In verse 4, the fruit of your womb and your crops and livestock will be blessed. In verse 5, your basket and kneading trough will be blessed. In verse 6, you will be blessed when you come in and when you go out. In verse 7, your enemies will be defeated before you. You will have an inheritance in the land he is giving you. In verse 8, everything we do will be blessed. In verse 9, we will be established as a holy people because we obey the commandments of God. In verse 10, people will fear us with holy fear and reverence because they see the hand of the Lord is on us. In verse 11, we will be abundantly prosperous. In verse 12, God will open the heavens to send rain and to bless all the work of our hands. In verse 13, we will lend money but borrow from none. We will be the head and not the tail if we pay attention and carefully follow the commands of the Lord, not turning to the left or the right.

Proverbs 4:4, 20-21, 6:23, 7:1-3. (ESV) We are to keep God's words and we will live, we will reign in life, His Words are light and life to those who find them. The life of God is in us. We are to write his word on our hearts. His commands and teachings will be as a lamp to light the way. His corrections will bring discipline to our lives. We must learn to listen to the voice of God. We must guard our thoughts; it is the wellspring of life; our thoughts shape our life.

Some features of obedience are a desire to obey, a decision to obey, and a determination to obey. These are all keys to obedience. Without wavering, we move forward on what we believe. We bring our desires into agreement when we walk on the word.

Each visit to Cuba, I visited an elderly man of ninety years, the father and grandfather of leaders. I had been in the area where he lived for some time and wanted to see and pray for him. One afternoon, on the back of a bicycle with a young man who spoke English, I visited. We had a lovely time, and later that day, I spoke with his grandson, the area church leader. He said to me, "This morning you prayed for my grandparents, and my grandfather fell on the floor, and God wonderfully touched him. What happened this afternoon when you prayed for my wife's grandfather?"

Shocked, I said, "I forgot to pray!"

We can be in the plan of God but just miss it. We can obey God, be in the right place at the right time, but miss the voice of God! I'm sure you will be pleased to know that a few days later, I visited and prayed for this dear man.

For Jesus, obedience to the Father was of supreme importance. The New Testament places special emphasis on Jesus's obedience. Jesus did exactly what his father commanded him to do (John 14:13, 31 ESV).

Every thought is to be brought into obedience, captive to Christ who is enthroned in our lives (2 Corinthians 10:4-5 ESV).

James 1:5-7 (TPT) says if anyone longs to be wise, ask God for wisdom, and he will give it! He won't see your lack of wisdom as an opportunity to scold you over your failures, but he will overwhelm your failures with his generous grace. Just make sure you ask, empowered by confident faith without doubting that you will receive. An ambivalent person believes one minute and doubts the next. Being undecided makes you become like the rough seas driven and tossed by the wind. You're up one minute and tossed down the next. When you are half-hearted and wavering, it leaves you unstable. Can you really expect to receive anything from the Lord when you're in that condition?

When we live in love and live by faith, with corresponding actions and words, we put the word in first place. When we decide to be healed or to fast, these become specific decisions that turn us around, as they become bits in our mouths like the horse (James 3:3 ESV).

We are to be determined. Are you determined to press in and obey? Jairus believed and acted as he was determined. Faith increases determination. As a synagogue leader, he wanted help from Jesus. The synagogue leaders were opposed to Jesus, but convinced that Jesus could help his daughter dying at home, he pleaded for help (Mark 5:35 ESV). He was determined to receive.

The night we visited the beautiful house, we drove on to the actual conference building outside the city. On that first night, the power failed! With flashlights, we found our way into the auditorium where about 30 women waiting. With no microphone, no translator, and no lights, we were all set for failure as other than the tiny flashlights, we were in the dark! But when we have the light of Jesus, none of us are in the dark! Wow, wonderful. As we laid hands on these ladies, they fell down and squatted on the floor, all connected to one another in a row, as in a trance. They were all just stuck there, all stuck together. Unforgettable! Determined to obey despite the power failure, despite the circumstances, we looked to Jesus who is Lord of the circumstances; we looked at Jesus and did what he said. These ladies were on the other side of our obedience.

GROUP WHO PRAYED

TRAVELLING TO THE NORTH

The Bible is full of people determined to obey. We looked at Abraham earlier, but there are others. I used to think about poor old Jeremiah and the struggle in his life until I watched the movie. That gave me a whole new perspective of his life. What a man of obedience he became, and what suffering amid opposition and persecution! All to do what God said.

The person's obedient response to God's word is a response of trust or faith. To hear God's word is to obey God's word. We are to listen and judge the word and do the work. To listen and do nothing is a sign of a deceived heart. Faith acts. To believe is to do!

In John 3:34, Jesus acted and spoke only as the Father directed. Because the father had sent him, he spoke the words of God. By living a life of obedience, Jesus showed himself to be the Savior. Jesus's work on the cross is viewed as a sacrifice of obedience (Romans 5:19 ESV).

Jesus said, "I am come to do your will, O God."
(—Hebrews 10:9 ESV)

He learnt obedience through the things suffered (Hebrews 5:8 ESV).

At every step, God is teaching us to obey. If we do not learn the lesson, we will not move on. A friend in Indiana said to us when difficult things happened, "This is just a test. If we don't pass the test, we have to sit it again."

As Jesus obeyed the Father's will, we are to be obedient to what he says. Obedience is to characterise our lives as disciples of Jesus. We are to deny the desires that once controlled us. Purified by faithful obedience, we are to be his people. To obey Jesus is the primary evidence that we love him and are his disciples. Our decision to obey the Lord is the key to understanding the spiritual reality of the Bible, as this action frees the Holy Spirit to teach and lead us.

What motivates us to obey God? Love for Jesus! If we love him, we do what he says.

India became a time of adventure, changing gear into new obedience at every turn. We stayed at a basic hotel, which became our home away from home, where every day a cockroach jumped on Treena's head. Scared of cockroaches, she found it horrifying that on this trip to Asia, her first, to have a large cockroach land on her head when waking or after showering. In answer to her cry, one man in the team prayed and rebuked the cockroaches, told them to get out of the room, and she never had another problem!

On the other side of his obedience, Treena sat. How happy she became to have the problem solved. Yes, we still can have issues, but when we pray, God sorts them out and solves them!

OUR SPECIAL FRIENDS FROM ALLENTOWN PA WHO BLESSED THE PEOPLE

No one can walk with God without obedience. Moses visited the pharaoh in obedience to the word of God. His obedience saved the entire race of Israelites (Exodus 4-5 ESV). He led the people of Israel out of slavery and bondage. Paul said he must obey the heavenly vision. After his conversion, obedience became a mark of his life. Ruth obeyed Naomi and released God's word (Ruth 1-4 ESV). Esther obeyed Mordecai, and God's people were saved (Esther 2-10, 2:19, 4:12-16 ESV).

We are to be obedient to the voice of God, through the written word and the spoken word. In Genesis 26:5 Amplified Bible, Abraham obeyed the voice of God, the charge of God, the commandments of God, the statutes of God, the laws of God, and we must do so too (Deuteronomy 4:5-6, 9, 6:3-5, Exodus 19:5 ESV). We are to be careful to observe God's words, for this will be our wisdom and understanding as it was for Moses. We are to keep God's word in the forefront of our thinking.

His words bring us life, for God will teach us and speak to us if we hold fast to his words. We are to pay attention and listen closely, consent and submit to these words, keeping them in the centre of our hearts, not letting them depart from our sight. As thoughts shape our lives, let's guard our hearts and choose to control those thoughts (Joshua 1:8, Proverbs 4:4 ESV).

In Luke 1:38 (ESV), we are to submit to God's authority as Mary did. We should submit our plans and future to God's will. We are to prefer God's will above our own.

As it says in John 2:5 (ESV), we must learn to practise instant obedience. Whatever God tells us to do, we should do. We must be teachable to be fruitful.

John 7:17 (ESV) says we should be determined to obey the Lord and align our will with his will to receive an understanding of his word. We are to understand that God chose us, and we were set apart by the Holy Spirit to live lives of obedience to Jesus Christ.

It says 1 John 2:3-6 (ESV) that we should know, recognise, and understand that obedience is the first evidence of love for God, and only those who obey and are learning to live like Jesus really know and love him. We are to discern (daily by experience) that we are coming to know him—to perceive, recognise, understand, and become better acquainted with him. If we keep (bear in mind, observe, practise) his teachings (precepts and commandments). Whoever says I know him—I perceive, recognise, understand, and am acquainted with him—but fails to keep and obey his commandments (teachings) is a liar. The truth (of the gospel) is not in him. But he who keeps (treasures) his word —who bears in mind his precepts, who observes his message in its entirety—truly in him has the love of and for God been perfected (completed, reached maturity). By this, we may perceive and know and recognise and be sure we are in him. Whoever says he abides in him, as a personal debt, ought to walk and conduct himself in the same way in which he walked and conducted himself.

OBEDIENCE AFFECTS OUR SPIRITUAL LIFE

A life of obedience to God is the fruit of faith (James 2:21-26 ESV).

Obedience affects our relationships with others. It will fill our lives with his love. Obedience is almost a dirty word as everyone wants to do their own thing; no one wants to be told what to do. Yet Jesus only did and said what the Father showed and told him.

One night in Cuba, I became extremely tired after ministering for twenty-four days without a day off. There seemed to be a problem to get an interpreter for the evening service. As the dramatic performance proceeded, I suggested to the senior pastor that I have a night off. But no, determined, he insisted the interpreter and I speak. She also suggested we have the night off, but to no avail. After consideration, he said, "If you don't feel to have an altar call, that's okay!" We had the drama, and I got up to speak. I looked at the time, 10:00 p.m., and thought they're all tired. They were all up 'til 3:00 a.m. the night before with New Year! They don't need this! I listened to the voice of my human reasoning. Yes, I spoke for twenty minutes, said lovely things, but really said nothing, then I prayed and sat down. The moment I sat down, I knew I had done the wrong thing! The next day the senior pastor asked me, "What happened to you last night?" He knew I should have had a call for prayer. He knew what God wanted! I missed hearing the voice of God. I repented. I think you would say, "But that's tough. He told you you didn't need to have the altar call."

Yes, I obeyed him because I felt tired, but in my spirit, I looked for a way out! It must be wholehearted obedience, a pure sacrifice.

When we change gear, stop listening to the Lord, we begin to reverse! Disobedience, the opposite to obedience, takes us backwards, reversing not necessarily to go where we want!

From Greek, disobedience is *apistia*, *apisteo*, *apieitha* (Strong's Bible Concordance).

Vine's definition is the condition of being unpersuadable, it implies obstinacy, obstinate rejection of the will of God, hearing amiss, a refusal to hear, is the effect of the condition of failing or refusing to hear (Vine's Expository Dictionary).

God has spoken in the scriptures. Disobedience to God's word comes from a sinful heart, a heart that will not trust God. Obedience comes from a heart that trusts God. If God's people obey him, they find the blessings he yearns to give. If they disobey, believers receive judgement and necessary discipline (1 Samuel 15:20-23; Isaiah 1:18-20; Ephesians 2:2 ESV).

The Bible views disobedience as a failure to hear and do God's word (Psalm 81:11 TPT). Israel is a nation that failed to listen to God and did not obey (Jeremiah 7:13 ESV). Jesus warned he that hath ears to hear, let him hear (Matthew 11:15 ESV).

Some kinds of disobedience are ignorance, wrong information, misunderstanding, and rebellion or stubbornness. Nadab and Abihu deliberately disobeyed the Lord. The result of them offering unholy fire, they died (Leviticus 10:1-3 ESV).

There is always a price to pay for disobedience. When we disobey, we shut our ears to God's word. We no longer listen or act, we become careless, and the next step is *sin*! Disobedience causes us to lose confidence in God. As we are to have a fidelity and confidence to believe that he will not fail and cannot fail, it comes out of our fellowship with him.

Some examples of failure to obey:

Adam, the first man, brought sin and disobedience, and it cost him his future (Genesis 3). Though Moses led the people of God into the promised land, when God said, "Speak to the rock," Moses did what he had done in the past and hit the rock. When there is deliberate disobedience, it is costly; it cost Moses his future! God punished him for disobedience, and he could not enter the promised land (Numbers 20:11-13 ESV). But we must be careful to do what God says and not rely on his previous words, which may bring us into disobedience.

Moving backwards can be unintentional or intentional! Failure to obey brings a curse; obedience brings a blessing. We reap what we sow, and the effects go on and on. There are many examples in the Bible of moving backwards, of going into reverse, even of accelerating in reverse, sometimes without fully realising the consequences.

Adam brought the curse of sin and death upon all mankind. Because of his deliberate disobedience in eating the fruit, he caused the very life of God to be cut off from him. It ended the intimate friendship, communication, and relationship he had enjoyed with God. When he turned from God and listened to his wife, he chose death rather than life, the way of his disobedience. Because of Adam's sin, all people are now born with sin, not the nature of God; sin separates from God (Romans 5:19 ESV).

King David—the faithful servant of the Lord who wrote psalms, who had an intimate relationship with God, loved God, and saw God do marvelous things—disobeyed God! He lusted after a woman, the wife of one of his mighty men. He committed adultery with her and then made sure her husband Uriah died unprotected in the battle's front, murdering him. Nathan, the prophet, came to him and confronted him with the sin. He repented before God but paid the price as the child Bathsheba bore died (2 Samuel 11-12 ESV).

When Saul, king of Israel, rebelled against the Lord, God rejected him as king. As he only repented to Samuel, not to the Lord, he blamed others for the sin. Saul did not destroy everything from the battle; he chose to be disobedient. God became angry with Saul, who lied to Samuel and did not take responsibility for his own actions "For to obey is better than sacrifice." Saul lost his inheritance because of his sin. His disobedience brought God's judgement. Rebellion is as the sin of witchcraft, divination, and stubbornness as the sin of idolatry (1 Samuel 13, 15:22-23 ESV).

When God told him to go to Nineveh, Jonah travelled in the opposite direction. Fear of man caused him to run away (Jonah 1 ESV).

Peter denied Jesus in the courtyard after they arrested Jesus, and when asked if he followed Jesus, he lied (Luke 22:54-62 ESV). Yet we are vulnerable if we stop listening, stop obeying. It is so important that we spend time with the Lord as disobedience can be gradual and insidious.

Some areas of deliverance are needed because of failure to obey.

> Behold I set before you life and prosperity, death and destruction. I set before you blessings and curses . . .

> We have before us life and death, it commands us to love the Lord our God and walk in His ways.
> (—Deuteronomy 30:15, 19 ESV)

Exodus 20 (ESV) speaks of the Ten Commandments, and in verses 3 and 4, there is the punishment on the children to the third generation because of idolatry. This verse says, "You shall worship the Lord your God and him, only will you serve." We are to have no other Gods.

A well-known preacher said the second we say no to prayer and say we are too tired or we don't feel like it, the real us becomes an idol worshipper because we are putting the self in the place of God. We have submitted to the lower nature, and our flesh has taken the place of God.

Deuteronomy 18:10-12 (ESV), "Let no one be found among you who sacrifices his son and daughter in the fire or who practices divination, sorcery, telling the future, interprets omens, engages in witchcraft, casts spells is a medium or spiritualist or consults the dead" (Leviticus 18:21, 20:6, 27 ESV).

Deuteronomy 28 (ESV) is the chapter of blessings and curses. Verses 1-14 deal with the blessings we come under when we walk in obedience, and verses 14-68 deal with the curses that come from disobedience to the Lord. If we have been involved in any of the following, we come under a curse.

This long list includes stealing, lying, not tithing, bribery, murder, pride, adultery, sexual immorality, bestiality, disobedience to God's word, stubbornness, rebellion, self-will, deceitfulness, idolatry, homosexuality, dishonour of parents, flattery, false teachers, preachers, assault of neighbours, gossip.

Indications of curses affecting our lives can be family and marriage breakdown and alienation, repeated and chronic sickness, illness with no known cause, hereditary infections, cancers, poverty, defeat, humiliation, barrenness, unfruitfulness, a tendency to miscarry, and reproductive disorders, we are the tail and not the head, oppression and failure, God's disfavor, frequent accidents and disasters, psychiatric disorders, confusion, mental and emotional illness, a history of suicides and unnatural and untimely deaths.

People have often said to me Christians cannot have curses because Jesus has delivered us from the curse at the cross. A pastor asked me one night, "Don't we get it all at conversion?" Yes, legally, I believe that is true, and it would be wonderful if we experienced all Jesus has for us when we are born again, but the reality is different for many believers.

ALIPIO AND OLGA

We had an amazing meeting in Cuba, where the power of God flowed, and we had prayed for everyone in the church. I turned to the musician on the keyboard, who had been busy throughout the ministry time, and said to him, "Would you like us to pray for you?"

"Yes," he said.

He stood, and we gathered around him. Though we prayed and prayed and prayed, it seemed like nothing was happening. God showed me to break generational ties and the curses of witchcraft and idolatry affecting his life. After I did this, the power of God came, and he was free. God sovereignly touched him. The leadership told me afterwards that, for generations, his family had been involved in witchcraft and idolatry. He thought he experienced freedom, but the effects of the curses go on and on. It's like a tree that has been chopped down. It keeps on sprouting fresh shoots, and we have to keep on taking the axe and chopping them out.

For there is no curse without a cause!

Worship of false Gods (Exodus 20:1-5 ESV) brings a generational curse and is spiritual adultery. Now we have another daunting list of involvement in occult or objects used for this purpose: acupressure, acupuncture, astral projection, hypnosis, martial arts, levitation, mind control, mind dynamics, touch healing, parakinesis, table-tipping, telekinesis, witchcraft, tarot, Ouija boards, palm-reading, divination, fortune-telling, lucky symbols, iridology, ESP, clairvoyance, hearing voices, horoscopes, reading stars, use of crystals, tea leaves, water-divining, communication with the spirit realm and the like, various moral and ethical sins, disrespect for parents, all forms of oppression and injustice, acknowledging and worshipping false gods, all forms of illicit and unnatural sex, anti-Semitism, legalism, apostasy, carnality, theft, perjury, robbing God, authority figures, self-imposed curses, soulish talk, soulish prayers.

In my own life, I suffered for many years with various types of pain and sickness, which continued on and on, one thing after another. With repeated unexplained sickness and pain, I kept going to the specialist to have tumors removed, burnt out of my bladder! It had become very horrible, the pain and suffering! Though gravely concerned as eight of these things had just been removed, with a high chance of recurrence, I arrived at church that morning, saying to the Lord, "Lord, I want some prayer today for healing or deliverance from whatever is necessary to remove the cause." I waited at the front at the close of the service for ministry. I wanted prayer from a particular person who moved in deliverance and words of knowledge. Finally, he came and prayed for me. He saw a picture of a huge dagger over my life and said he saw a curse of death and hell over me and Satan had been trying to kill me. While on the floor under the power of God, he had a word of knowledge. This almost embarrassed him to give, and finally, he said, "Did your mother not want you? Did she try to abort you?"

I said I did not think so, but I knew what God had showed him, and I said, "Many years ago, I had a pregnancy terminated, from which I had repented."

He prayed and broke the curses, which had come upon me over my life because of this, and I experienced freedom. That day Jesus healed me and the problems ended. The effects of the curses had gone on and on in my life, and I did not realise. We reap what we sow. If we break God's laws, there are consequences.

John 8:32-36 (ESV) tells us that Jesus speaks of the freedom that he brings. In Joshua 2 is the story of Rahab the prostitute, set free because of her acceptance of the spies.

John 11:38 (ESV) speaks of Lazarus being raised from the dead. Jesus called Lazarus forth from the tomb. He said, "Lazarus, come out," and Lazarus came out, wrapped in the grave clothes. Healed, delivered, resurrected, and made whole in one action, he still had to have the grave clothes unwrapped. They bound him, even though the miraculous had happened to him. Yet it was only when they took off the grave clothes that they set him free. Wrapped tight around him, he could not undo them. That is what it is like for some of us when Jesus comes into our lives and we are born again. We become a new creation, but often we need to be untied, released from the burial clothes around our lives. Because Jesus took all our sins, sickness, curses at the cross, legally, we are free. Jesus gave Lazarus new life, but he still had to be unwrapped and set free. Isn't this the same for you and me?

> The law of the spirit of life has set me free from the law of sin and death.
> (—Romans 8:2 ESV)

I'm set free by the spirit of God. The life of Jesus is in us, but the effects of the curses go on and on, and we must cut them off and walk in freedom. Yes, Jesus legally took all our sins at the cross, but like Lazarus, some of us wait to be unwrapped and be fully free.

We can only set people free if we are free ourselves. We must move on so we can teach others to move on. We are to dig their roots out, not cut them out! We must dig them out (Revelation 12:11 ESV).

After a session on the curses, we ministered to the students of the Kathmandu Bible school. How fantastic to see them delivered and set free in the name of Jesus to go forth to minister deliverance.

LEADERSHIP NEPAL TRAINING CENTRE

Our friend Nona, through her faithfulness and love, has changed the lives of thousands of believers across the Himalayan Ranges. As a substantial giver to an international book ministry, she has a heart to see transformation. Integral in the release of thousands of sets of books in their own languages, she has caused this to happen! We place them into the hands of people attending our conferences. By faith, we have taken and given these books across this desperate region where they have needed deliverance and discipleship-teaching.

NONA DANI AND ELLA

Faith with the word and action casts out fear, unbelief, and disobedience.

The result is the blessings of God, the presence of God, the power of God, and the glory of God. Let's move forward again on the green light, changing gear to speed up God's purpose.

SUPPLEMENTARY QUESTIONS

Do I have this kind of faith? How does it manifest in my life?

Do I hear God's voice? Do I do what he says?

Do I have any areas of unbelief and fear in my life?

Surrender these today to the spirit of God, repent, and ask him to remove them.

RELATIONSHIP CHANGES OUR GEAR

FAITH AND OBEDIENCE BRING RELATIONSHIP

Many years ago, our marriage failed, and it separated me from Kevin. I took our two small children and all our belongings, left the town we were living in, and moved to the far south of New Zealand, to the city of my birth, where my family lived. Done with the marriage, I said, "Unless he changes, I want nothing more to do with the marriage!"

Six months passed, I worked two nights a week and lived happily and peacefully in a small apartment in that city. I had enough, enough of bickering, strife, division, and difficulties! In the following months, Kevin wrote to me twice, asking for a reconciliation. I said, "No!"

Many Christians came and tried to tell me what to do! They tried to do God's job for him! They told me, "How can you love God and be baptised in the Holy Spirit and yet leave your husband?"

God had it all in hand. I had two very unsettling dreams, which proved to be the beginning of God stepping into the situation. That Christmas, nine months after the separation, I attended a convention, and there, God spoke. At the seminars, I heard that if we want to know the plan and purpose of God, we are to obey him. God spoke to me. "Do you love me?"

I said, "Yes, Lord."

He asked again, "Do you love me?"

I said, "Yes, Lord."

Then again, he asked, "Do you love me?"

I was getting a little tired of it by the third time, and like Peter, I said, "Lord, you know that I love you!"

He said, "If you love me, obey my word."

I replied, "Lord, I'm trying to."

He said, "Love your husband!"

I said, "Lord, I can't do that. That is impossible. I just don't have any love left for him. It's finished. It didn't work. It was hopeless. Anyway, God, he doesn't want us anymore."

God spoke. "You can't do it, but I can. I delight to do the impossible! Love him by faith. Will to love him, and I will love him through you. Leave him to me. He is mine. Take your hands off him, and live by my word. Allow me to love him through you. Will you be a channel of my love?"

I said, "Yes, Lord, I will obey your word."

It was at that convention that as I received ministry each day, God did a tremendous work of physical and emotional healing. I wrote to Kevin, asking him to consider meeting with me to discuss a reconciliation. Almost a year had passed, and he was happy living in Hamilton. Shocked, it took some negotiation before he agreed to meet with me in another city in New Zealand, halfway between where we both were living. Finally, several weeks later, we met. I went to the meeting, saying,

"God, you do this. You bring this reconciliation. I will love him by faith, even though I feel nothing! Lord, love him through me. I will trust you, God, in this."

He came to the meeting, saying, "I am what I am. Unless she has changed, there is no hope, it is finished!"

God did it. Later Kevin shared that he met a woman who was completely changed; this "new person" loved and cared for him in a way he had never experienced previously in the marriage. It reconciled the marriage. Shortly after this, we moved to that city where we had met, and God gave us a new marriage, not something healed with scars, but new. God does all things well.

KEVIN AND DENISE

> Then He said unto them, If any one would come after me, let him deny himself and take up his cross daily and follow Me. For whoever wants to save his life will lose it, but whoever loses his life for My sake will save it.
> (—Luke 9:23 ESV)

Yes, we are to lose sight of ourselves, give up our rights, give up our own self-interests and replace them with God's interests, deny ourselves. If we want such a relationship with Jesus, that our lives are changed and people who we touch become changed, then this is the key.

> He was led as a lamb to the slaughter
> yet He did not open His mouth.
> (—Isaiah 53:7 ESV)

He said nothing! He refused to reply. God asks for our self denial, complete dedication, willing obedience, total commitment, total surrender, to die daily, not just once, but also to take up our cross daily. We are to follow him. The cross symbolises total commitment. That's all. That's everything. Cross-bearing is a willingness to suffer and die for the Lord's sake. The picture in this passage is of a man who is already condemned. It requires him to carry his own cross to the place of execution. This man is one who did not answer back, who accepted whatever was done to him, who suffered and died for us. This man was Jesus, the Son of the Living God. We are to die daily to follow him, not just to die once, but also to keep on dying.

It's painful to die. We die alone in total surrender!

A pastor with a big church in China is a heart-rending example of surrender. Many years ago, the government came to him and told him he must register and become part of the official government church or close his church. He refused and continued to serve the Lord and his church, and the police took him to prison. For many years, he suffered re-education through torture and indoctrination. His wife and family could visit him every few months as the prison was only a few hours away.

After several years, because he refused to recant or compromise, he was moved to another prison in the north, far from his family. He was very sad as he loved his dear wife and longed to see her. Now she could only come once a year as it took many days of travel to reach him. The years passed, and he worked long hours in the coal mines, suffering ridicule, deprivation, and degradation. He could have left at any time and gone home to his family; he could have left at any stage if he had chosen to deny Jesus. But he chose to stay. He chose to follow Jesus without compromise.

Year after year, his wife came to visit him. For sixteen years, his wife came to see him, and on the seventeenth year, when the time came for her visit, there stood his mother!

"Where is my dear wife?" he anxiously asked. He was pleased to see his mother, but how he longed to see his wife.

"She is sick and unable to come," his mother said.

Another year passed, and he waited for his wife to come, but this time his sister came.

"Your wife was sick again," she said.

He was sad. He was longing to see his wife. The next year, his nineteenth year in prison, the visit came and went, and no one came to see him. He was sad. How he longed for some news. What was happening to his wife, to his family, to his church? Finally, the day drew near for his release. He was praying, "Lord, let me go home. Please, Lord, overrule, don't let them send me to another area. Lord, you are the God of the impossible, please send me home."

The day came, and they called him to the prison governor, and he was told he could go back home. He was so thankful, so eager. He ran to the train. He couldn't wait. At last, he was going home. At last, he was going to see his wife. His heart was eager with longing to see her. As the train travelled the hundreds of miles, and the days passed, his excitement grew. At last, here was his city. He hurried to the bus. There was his street. He ran. He stumbled on the rough cobblestones. Nothing had changed. It was almost as though time had stood still. He was home. He passed the policeman at the ground floor door of his building. He climbed the steps, one floor past the offices, two floors past the church.

Ah! Here he was at last. He burst through the door into the apartment. There was his sister, who rose eagerly to greet him. He looked around anxiously and rushed into the next room. There was his aged mother dying of cancer. He turned to his sister. "Where is my dear wife? Where is my wife? Is she out visiting, out evangelizing?"

"No," she said. "She died last year!"

It stunned him, and he wept and wept. "My wife! My dear wife! How I longed to see her."

He could have left prison on denial of faith in Jesus. He could have gone home to his wife. He loved Jesus and served twenty years in prison. He lost twenty years of his life, lost his wife. He gave his all for Jesus. This church has continued to exist and grow. Today there are over one thousand people who fellowship at this unregistered house church. The government continues to oppress and persecute them; the pastor is now in heaven. Soldiers came and took away all the gifts received from the Western church, Bibles, a sound system, study materials, and equipment. He told them, "You can break up the building. You can take away all we have. You can take me to prison and even kill me, but never will I deny my Jesus!" (Bold as a Lamb.)

2 Corinthians 4:1l says, (ESV) For we who live are always being given over to death for Jesus' sake, so that the life of Jesus also may be manifested in our mortal flesh.

Except a grain of wheat fall into the ground and die it remains alone, only when it dies do many seeds come forth. (—John 12:24 ESV)

It's the same for us; it's only in dying that we live.

When we die, God does something new, not just in us, but also in our ministry, in our entire lives. It is a resurrection, a whole new thing. You see, it is not what we do for God that matters; it is what we allow him to do in us, that they will see the beauty of Jesus in us. He wants to burn out the rubbish. He wants a relationship with us. He wants us to trust completely, to lean on and rely totally on him.

FAITH + OBEDIENCE + RELATIONSHIP = VISION

When we have faith, we develop a relationship with the Lord. As we learn to obey God, we develop in our relationship. If we were slaves, we would not need this relationship as we would do what we were told without question all the time. We are not slaves; we are sons and daughters of the Living God. When we were born again and became a new creation, we were born into the family of God. When a mother births a baby, a son or daughter arrives to become a new member of the family. There is great rejoicing at the new birth. It's the same when we were born again. The angels rejoiced. When a baby is born, we must feed the baby. If we don't feed the baby, it dies. When it gets older, we teach a child to feed itself, and we need to know how to feed ourselves, as without food, our spiritual life will die.

Increased faith speaks of increased relationship.

> We are heirs of the Father joint heirs with the Son.
> (—Romans 8:17 ESV)

We are children of God, joint heirs with Jesus, heirs of all that God has the right to. There is tremendous possibility in the relationship.

The driver shared with us he had bad headaches. Every morning he suffered terrible pain in his head. On enquiry, he admitted his wife was the priestess at the family shrine on their property. After relationships with his wife, his head ached badly! He asked for prayer. His wife came the following day, and we prayed for her. She became very stiff and would not give her life to Jesus. We would have stopped praying when she said no, she did not want to receive Jesus and be born again, but the leaders said, "No, keep praying. This is just demons!"

A group kept praying, and they said they saw her body gradually respond. Many hours later, she was slowly responding. Finally, all demonic activity ceased. But now there was great consternation! This beautiful young woman could not walk. Crippled, she sat there; her legs useless! The team prayed and prayed until, finally, the lady shared that, as a baby, when they dedicated her to the gods and anointed her for her task, the priest cut the tendons on her legs, and since then, she had walked through demonic power! What a challenge! We needed more prayer until she was healed. Hours later, this young woman not only walked, but also became a child of God who healed and set her free.

HUSBAND BEING PRAYED FOR HEALING OF HEADACHES

Relationships come in two categories: relationship by association and relationship by blood tie. Many people have a relationship by association, but what God wants is a relationship by blood tie. The blood tie removes the servant/slave mentality and brings us into the son/daughter/heir relationship. The son or daughter relationship has an expectation of inheritance.

Ask yourself, which of these do you have? How hungry are you for God? Our hunger will determine our relationship.

In New Zealand, there is a very pretty little native bird called the fantail. It is black and grey with an orange breast and a fantail. This bird flits about, flying around and up and down onto tree branches. It stops and starts all the time tweeting and following you as you walk. It is extremely friendly and comes to within arms' reach, flying round and round, sometimes in front and sometimes behind.

One day, while walking along an estuary area, one of these little birds followed me, flying all around me, and God showed me that many of us are just like this little bird in our relationship with him. We have no sense of direction and move along almost at whim, flitting here and there from thing to thing, with no plan, no purpose, no direction, a beautiful creation, yet for what? You have its companionship but no relationship. The fantail flies around, following, going ahead, going round and round. God showed me we are like the fantail; we follow for a while, we are earnest, but then we stop and start. Distracted, we pause as we flit around, and we follow again. We seek God for a while, but something comes along and distracts us. We stop, we start, we have good intentions to pray or go to a prayer meeting, but we get waylaid, sidetracked. The fantail follows us along, lingering, not catching up, always elusive.

NEW ZEALAND FANTAIL

There are two things this makes me think of: independence and dependence. *Collins Dictionary* defines *independence* as "the state or quality of being independent; free from the control of another power in action and judgement; autonomous; not dependent on anything," just like the fantail. *Collins Dictionary* defines dependence as "which is to put trust in; to rely on; a person who depends on another person for support; reliance, trust, confidence; being dependent for help; something or someone upon which one relies."

Jesus wants us not to walk behind him, following at a distance, not to stop and start or be elusive, only partly committed, on again, off again. He wants a relationship with us, in which we can depend on him, for he is utterly reliable. He wants us to walk with him hand in hand, not to follow in his footsteps, where he has trod, but hand in hand alongside him. As his spirit leads us, we depend and are reliant on him. The beauty of Jesus is to be seen in us (Philippians 2 ESV). We are even to lean on him as it says in Song of Solomon 8:5, "Who is this coming up from the desert leaning on the arm of her beloved?" He wants a love relationship with us.

Are you like the fantail? Does your relationship need a fresh touch? Are you flitting around without purpose? Do you know the plan of God? Do you have a vision? Can God trust you?

> If you love me, keep my commandments.
> (—John 14:15 ESV)

Obedience is a key to an intimate relationship. Does he come to you? Are you willing to pay the price? Are you willing to be what God wants you to be? Do you want such a relationship with the Holy Spirit that people know you have been with Jesus?

> And I will lead her out into the desert and speak tenderly to her . . . I will betroth you to Me for ever.
> (—Hosea 2:14, 19 ESV)

Jesus wants to betroth us to him forever. Jesus is our direction. His Holy Spirit wants to come to each of us and reveal Jesus to us.

Are you hungry for more of God? The Holy Spirit wants to come to you. He is here right now to touch you. Are you hungry?

In that beautiful love song, Song of Solomon, I saw things I had never realised before. Isn't it wonderful the way God brings new revelation when we read the scriptures? These chapters speak of the relationship of the beloved and the lover, which goes from immaturity and fervency to maturity and intimacy.

In the Bible, we all know what being intimate means. We give our entire selves to another, our lover, our husband. But in the world, to be intimate is to give yourself to your partner at the time! It's God's value regarding love we are talking about here, "intimate love." This love and intimacy will cause passion to rise in our lives like the lover and the bride, the beloved. Passion has fervor, adoration, intensity, fervency, excitement, and emotion. Jesus, the bridegroom, wants this relationship with you and me.

Song of Solomon 1:3-4 (ESV) says, "Your name is like perfume poured out," like ointment is the name of Jesus, our beloved, our lover. Take me away with you." We are to ask the Lord to draw us on, to take us away with him. He wants to do it.

Psalm 91:1 (ESV) says we are to "dwell in the secret place of the Most High, to dwell under the shadow of the Almighty."

Our relationship with him will cause us to arise and come to Jesus, like the stag on the rugged hills, hills of difficulties (Song of Solomon 2:8, 14, 17 ESV). We will have difficulties, but just like that stag that bounds nimbly, he will be with us, and we will bound nimbly with sure feet over the difficulties. We are to come to the secret place of the rock alone with him. He promises to give us hind feet in high places.

Chapter 3 verses 1–3 (ESV) speaks of how the beloved sought for her lover but did not find him all night long on her bed. He withdrew because she did not go with him. Then she searched for him until she found him. Through withdrawal, he drew her on (verse 4). So it is for us. We must take care that God does not withdraw from us because we do not go on with him. When he speaks to us and calls us, we are to come with him wherever he would take us. Just go anywhere, do anything. Should he withdraw, we are to search and search diligently until we find him. The withdrawal is to lead us on into a deeper relationship with him.

> God is a God who hides Himself.
> (—Isaiah 45:15 ESV)

God promises to reveal himself to those who seek for him (Jeremiah 33:3, Matthew 7:7 ESV).

We must be hungry for him, that we will know him as he is. That is my prayer, that I may know him more. When we are hungry, we get more hungry. I don't know about you, but I know that when I fast, I am not hungry, and often I don't even want food. Yet when I eat, the more I eat; often the more hungry I get. Think about it! The more we feed on the word, the more we will want to feed on the word, and it works too in reverse. The less we feed on the word, the less we want to feed on the word.

Chapter 3:6 (ESV) speaks of "coming up from the desert perfumed with myrrh." Myrrh and incense speak to us of the fragrance of suffering. We come from the desert experiences perfumed with suffering. There is no other way to a deepening relationship with Jesus but the way of the cross. The alabaster bottle had to be broken and the fragrance poured out (Matthew 26:7 ESV).

The cross symbolises total commitment. That's all; that's everything. He wants our total obedience; nothing less is good enough. To see a move of God, there must be total obedience. God wants a holy people, set apart for him.

We shall be holy, holy unto the Lord.
(—1 Peter 1:15 ESV)

When God did a work in me, it was painful. It was a death experience, but out of it, God brought forth a new me. Diagnosed with a fast-growing cancer, the devil tried to kill me, to kill the purpose and plan of God. After three operations and radiation . . . (more about in *Heavenly Kaleidoscope* or *Endless Safari*)

Sometime later on that radiation table, I looked up at that great big beam above me, and I cried out to the Lord and said, "Lord Jesus, use this beam for your good. Do whatever you want in my life. I yield to you. I surrender all. Cut off all the rubbish! Do an additional work in me. I'm yours, Lord."

As tears poured down my cheeks, God took me at my word. As though I died, another person emerged, sold out to Jesus. When we die, God does a whole new thing, not a Band-Aid covering a wound. He does all things well. A new life and ministry was to emerge! This was the myrrh of suffering.

Song of Songs 2:10 (TPT) Can you not discern this new day of destiny breaking forth around you? The early signs of my purposes and plans are bursting forth. The budding vines of new life are now blooming everywhere. The fragrance of their flowers whispers, "There is change in the air." Arise, my love, my beautiful companion, and run with me to the higher place. For now is the time to arise and come away with me.

Yes, there was a change in the air. After the battle, a new day of destiny dawned, and God spoke, telling me to go to Cuba!

In chapter 4:6 (ESV), it says, "Until the day breaks and the shadows flee, I will go to the mountain of myrrh and to the hill of incense." I will go the way of the cross, a way of suffering and death, and I go to it joyfully. I choose to go there. Our walk with Jesus, it's always a choice. It is different for each of us, but there is the way of the cross for all of us. You can't embrace my cross, nor I yours. Should we seek to, this would be legalism. It is costly.

In verse 8 (ESV), he says to her, "Come with me my bride, come with me to a new walk a more mature walk, and be my coheir." The result is she entrusts herself to him, no matter what the cost, amid lions and leopards! We are to come away with him through the difficult places.

Daily I proclaimed the word over my shoulder and my body. Daily I exercised and forced my arm to move. Daily I fought the devil who came with mind control and verbal assault. Finally, eight months later, the shoulder was free, and in the strength of the Lord, I went to Cuba! Nothing is impossible to our God. Hallelujah!

The beloved, she is not subservient, she is the coheir. That is to be our relationship. Jesus takes us to new levels of warfare and assault. There is a fight of faith against lions and leopards, devouring animals. Though there is much to fight against, Jesus is with us. He says he will never leave us, never forsake us (Song of Solomon 4:8 ESV). Maturity is now coming for the beloved, my bride.

There has been the cold, the bitter north wind of winter, and now the south wind of blessing comes. Jesus says, "I am overwhelmed with your devotion, you have ravished my heart" You reach into my heart. With one flash of your eyes, I am undone by your love, my beloved, my equal, my bride. You leave me breathless—I am overcome by merely a glance from your worshipping eyes, for you have stolen my heart. I am held hostage by your love and by the graces of righteousness shining upon you (Song of Solomon 4:9 TPT).

God says this to us. Testing brings three things: withdrawal by the Lord, we just don't hear him like we did; rejection by those around us; and seduction (Song of Solomon 4:16; 5:5-7, 16 TPT).

Our attitudes must stay right even in these circumstances. After we have stayed true to Jesus, he validates us. We live for his pleasure, not our own. We are to reap the harvest. Don't think it will be easy. It is difficult (6:5; 7:10-12 ESV).

Verse 7 (ESV) says, "They beat me, they bruised me, they took away my cloak, those watchmen of the walls!" The cloak speaks of the covering. The people you think will love and support you, the ones you think will be thrilled at what God is doing, often become jealous and envious and try to bring you down with gossip and criticism. Your attack does not always come from the world. The very place where you worship may bring assault! Rejection is painful, but we all have to die.

We must allow difficulties, persecution, and rejection to make us better, not bitter!

On the return of the team from Cuba on the second trip, there were lots of issues as those who went had difficulty accepting the move of God. They questioned and denied some of the wonderful things God had done, and as a result, it was like there were bricks and blocks and boulders that they could not climb over. Criticism arose, and it became very difficult. After the glory was the pain! With little understanding in the fellowship of the degree of glory, or the extent of the move of God, the rejection was considerable, and the pain continued. All these things work together for good to those who love God and are called according to his purpose. Suffering is to make us better, not bitter. Rejection makes us better, not bitter. We have to respond in the right way.

At the close of chapter 5, there is an amazing love statement in which the beloved speaks of the lover and her unwavering commitment despite all that had happened. We need to come into that place where we can say like Esther, "If I perish, I perish!"

> Though the fig tree should not blossom, nor fruit be on the vines, the produce of the olive fail and the fields yield no food, the flock be cut off from the fold and there be no herd in the stalls, yet I will rejoice in the LORD; I will take joy in the God of my salvation. GOD, the Lord, is my strength; he makes my feet like the deer's; he makes me tread on my high places. To the choirmaster: with stringed instruments.
> (—Habakkuk 3:17-19 ESV)

Finally, in Song of Solomon 5:16 (TPT), she says, "This is my lover, my friend." After we stand true to Jesus, he validates us. He brings us to maturity and sets the seal of his love upon us as his fire burns within us (Song of Solomon 8:6-7 ESV). We live for his pleasure, not our own. Song of Solomon 7:10-13 (ESV) tells us we are to reap the harvest. We are to go to the countryside with our lover Jesus and see if the vines have budded and to see the blossoms and the fruit. He brings us to maturity and sets the seal of his love upon us. We are the glory of our beloved and will reign with him as his most treasured possession. God speaks these words over us in his great love for us. We are to come up from the desert, leaning on the arm of our beloved, our lover, JESUS! We come from the difficulties from the dry places on the arms of our lover, the arms of Jesus.

> As the deer pants for streams of water, so my soul pants for You O God. My soul thirsts for God, for the living God.
> (—Psalm 42:1-2 ESV)

When can I go to meet with God? When can I behold the face of God? We are too long for the presence of God. These waters are living waters.

Jeremiah 23:23-24 (ESV) tells us that when we come into the presence of God, sometimes it takes time; sometimes it is like God is far away. God hides himself from us until he knows we are starving and he can trust us.

The word of God says that if we were to devote ourselves to seek him, to get close to him, if we will call to him, he will show us the hidden things, the mighty things, the things that he has prepared for those who love him. God hides himself, and we are to seek hard after him. As we seek him, we will be his people, and he will be our God. Our relationship is to be such that when we call on the Lord, he trusts us as a friend ((Jeremiah 30:21, Jeremiah 33:3 ESV).

God will only reveal himself to those who diligently seek him. He hides himself and will only reveal himself to us fully if he can trust us. God's love is a jealous love. He wants us to love him with all our hearts. Anything that we spend more time with than God is idolatry in our lives, and God wants first place.

> At each and every sunrise you will hear my voice as I prepare my *sacrifice of* prayer to you. Every morning I lay out the pieces of my life on the altar and wait *for your fire to fall upon my heart.*
> (—Psalm 5: 3 TPT)

> In the morning O Lord, You hear my voice, in the morning I lay my requests before You, and wait in expectation.
> (—Psalm 5:3 ESV)

Early in the morning, we are to rise and seek the Lord. If we want God's best, we must do it God's way and want God's best! It is a personal relationship with God, and that takes time, effort, and energy!

We cannot walk on someone else's relationship. Yesterday's blessings are no good for today. We are to seek God daily.

A wonderful story that spoke to me is a story told by Stormont, Smith Wigglesworth's son-in-law.

When Smith Wigglesworth stayed in our home once, he came down the stairs early one morning and told me, "God spoke to me on your bed."

"What did he say?" I asked.

He said, "Wigglesworth, I'm going to burn you all up 'til there is no more Wigglesworth, only Jesus."

Standing at the foot of our stairs, he raised his hands to heaven, and with tears running down his face, he cried, "O God, come and do it. I don't want them to see me anymore, only Jesus!"

Yes, he comes to burn us up.

Wigglesworth did not let 15 minutes go by on any day when he did not speak to God!

Is that how you and I live, that people would see Jesus when they see us? Our relationship should be such that when we call to God, he trusts us as a friend.

WIGGLESWORTH MEETING

Examples of this are David and Jonathan and the Three Musketeers. These were men who were committed to each other, who were faithful and served each other even unto death. David and Jonathan had a covenant with each other, a blood covenant that could not be broken. This speaks of a relationship that is more than these definitions imply.

To be a friend is to be friendly, to care, to help, to love.

Penguin's Dictionary says about friendship: "a person who is cheerful and comforting."

A friend is one who cares and loves you, no matter what the cost or the circumstances. There are no legal ties; it is a matter of choice. To have a friend, we must be a friend. Many years ago, I did of a lot of church-visiting, and in the process, I built a relationship over time with a very needy woman. I called at her house over many weeks, leaving gifts of eggs and vegetables from our garden, but each time I went to see her, she was not at home. Finally, I caught up with her, and we became friends. I spent many hours just listening to her as she poured out her heart. One day she shared with me, "You are my only friend!"

I thought about the implications of this. I was her only friend. In my scale of things, she was someone I visited to help and teach about Jesus, someone to whom I could show God's love, but for her, I was the one and only person who cared.

God wants to be our friend. In our relationship with the Lord, there is to be harmony, peace, concord, fellowship, and most of all intimacy. God wants to be intimate with us. To have a friend, we must spend time with that person. We do not rush into their house and talk, talk, talk, and then say goodbye. We do not treat them shabbily. If we did, we would soon not have a friend. No! We spend time with them. We try to help them and please them. We listen to them, and they listen to us.

With Moses, the friend of God, the Lord spoke face-to-face, friend to friend. God wants this relationship with us. We are his friends, and we come into his presence as soon as we talk to God. God knew Moses by name; he knew him in every way. When God called Moses, he came in the desert in a supernatural experience. In an encounter with God, his will became known (Exodus 3;3; 19:3 ESV). We often have to go to dry desert valleys to meet God. God births change in us in the desert places, and it is only when we come up out of the wilderness that God does new things. When God revealed himself in a burning bush in Exodus 3, the bush did not consume. God said to Moses, "Take off your shoes, the place where you are standing is holy ground."

Moses experienced the fire that changed his life forever. In Exodus 3:10 (ESV), the Lord commissioned Moses. After he had forty years in the desert as a nothing, a nobody, God came. From being a prince and a ruler in Egypt, now he looked after the sheep. When God came to him, he had to die to what he had been, not to a proud, arrogant, impetuous man but to one now humble.

The Holy Spirit revealed God to him, and it totally changed him. Moses died to the past, and God did something new. Delivered to deliver, the key is in his willingness. God couldn't do it unless he surrendered willingly. He said, "Who am I Lord?"

I'm nothing, Lord, nothing without you, Lord. God uses the weak to confound the wise (1 Corinthians 1:27 ESV).

Moses said, "Here I am" He yielded to the Lord, but he argued, showing he still had that part of the flesh (Exodus 3:4-13, 4:1 ESV). He had five excuses. And like me, I'm sure you will identify with them. "Who am I?" "I'm not ready!" "What will I say?" "They might not listen to me!" Fear of failure ruled him. "I can't speak well." (Exodus 4:10, 11 ESV) Have you said these to the Lord? Has he spoken, and you have used this smoke screen to hide behind?

When God called me, he gave me the passage in Jeremiah 1 (ESV), and I like to change it and make it say the following because that is the way God spoke to me through it. "Now the word of the LORD came to me, saying, 'Before I formed you in the womb, I knew you, and before you were born, I consecrated you. I have appointed you a prophet to the nations.'

"Then I said, 'Alas, LORD GOD! Behold, I do not know how to speak because I am only a woman.'

"But the LORD said to me, 'Do not say "I am only a woman" because everywhere I send you, you shall go, and all that I command you, you shall speak.'

"'Do not be afraid of them, for I am with you to deliver (rescue) you,' declares the LORD.

"Then the LORD stretched out his hand and touched my mouth, and the LORD said to me, 'Behold, I have put my words in your mouth.' See,

I have appointed you this day over the nations and over the kingdoms to pluck up and to break down, to destroy and to overthrow, to build and to plant.'"

Moses climbed the mountain up to God after the Lord called to him from the mountain and said, "This is what you are to say to the house of Jacob." After this, Moses obeyed and told the people and set before them all the words the Lord had commanded him to speak. They transmitted this to the people through the elders, and Moses returned to God with the people's response. We must do that. We are to go to God and get his instructions for situations, then go to others, build them up, and lead them on into an ever-deepening relationship with the Lord. As we are to train people to listen and obey, they will follow God's voice, which is what Moses did when he led the people. What an example!

Moses's faith came from his relationship with the Lord. Our faith and our obedience will come from our relationship. It won't just happen. He spent time with God hungry for more of God. In Exodus 33:9-11 (ESV), Moses would go into the tent, and God would come and speak with him face-to-face. As Moses had a history with God, God knew he could trust Moses. God knew he held first place in Moses's life, and he had taught Moses what to do in many difficult situations. God wants us to understand this.

Apologising, the pastor said, "I'm so sorry, the unbelievers all came in off the street, the power of God so amazing!"

They came in to look and stayed because they have seen nothing like this before. They stood there and watched. We could hardly move. They got in the way as the small church full of people became like a zoo! So it became difficult. Everyone looked at me, watched my every movement. Like at the zoo, I became an animal. Everyone watching open-mouthed; no one praying! Praying for people in the squash became almost impossible. I just wanted to escape and as quickly as possible! Fortunately, a passage ran along the side that led to the house, and we prayed there. I remember hating it so much! Such an unpleasant experience. Can you remember having an unpleasant experience when God is moving? How could it be so bad? So many people, so difficult, and so many onlookers! God moved so powerfully! Afterwards, tired and cross, God spoke. "How you can be so angry with what I did? If I make it like the zoo, then that's my problem, not yours! You are my weapon to bring my presence and power!" After that, what could I say? I repented!

Imagine facing the Red Sea at the front, and the Egyptian army chasing hard after you from behind. What would you think? Yet when Moses asked God what to do, God said, "Why are you crying out to me? Stretch out your hand over the sea to divide the water!"

Notice, though, that before Moses called out to God, he spoke by faith to the people. He said, "Stand firm, and you will see the deliverance the Lord will bring you today. The Egyptians you see today, you will never see again!"

There comes a moment in every relationship that calls for action. No better time! Moses obeyed, and the waters parted. He became the deliverer God called him to be (Exodus 14:15 ESV).

Imagine facing over a million people, moaning about food and water. The waters were bitter at Marah; the people needed food. Moses cried out to the Lord, and not only were the waters healed, but he also provided the manna and quail (Exodus 15-16).

Have you ever been in a desert, in the heat, in the dust and dryness? Your lips get dry, your tongue gets dry, your throat gets dry, and you cough, you sense thirst, and you can't swallow. The Israelites were not only thirsty, but once again, they were also moaning and complaining. Moses cried out to God, the God of miracles; he hit the rock, and it provided water (Exodus 17:1-7 ESV).

Moses found favor with God.

> Moses said to the Lord, "You say to me bring up this people: But You have not let me know whom you will send with me, Yet You said, I know you by name, and you have found favor in My sight."
> (—Exodus 33:12 ESV)

God knows us by name.

> I have summoned you by name.
> (—Isaiah 43:1 ESV)

He has called us, anointed us, appointed us just as he did Moses for his own special purpose, and he will give us the treasures of darkness (Isaiah 45:3). Why? How did Moses find favor? He found favor with God because of his relationship that came from his obedience and faith.

That zoo night, a woman present became our divine appointment. We were unaware of her presence in the service, but after the meeting, she returned home to her husband at their son's house where they visited. She told her husband, "You must have this woman" and told him of the meeting! As a result, this opened the door to the Guantanamo district and many other areas. We found out later that he had been saying, "Why should I have them? They are just women!"

THE WOMAN WHO OPENED UP
GUANTANAMO DISTRICT

Moses had a relationship. When the pillar of cloud descended, God met him in the tent face-to-face as a man meets with his friend. God spoke of Moses as "my servant Moses," and Moses listened carefully to God and did what he said (Exodus 33:9-11 (ESV), Exodus 24:18).

Numbers 12:3-8 [ESV] "Now Moses was a very humble man, more humble than anyone else on the face of the earth. At once the LORD said to Moses, Aaron and Miriam, come out to the Tent of Meeting, all three of you." So the three of them came out. Then the Lord came down in a pillar of cloud; he stood at the entrance to the tent and summoned Aaron and Miriam. When both of them stepped forward, he said, "Listen to my words: When a prophet of the LORD is among you, I reveal myself to him in visions. I speak to him in dreams. But this is not true of my servant Moses. He is faithful in all my house. With him, I speak face-to-face, clearly and not in riddles. He sees the form of the Lord . . ."

> Now therefore, if I have found favor in your sight, please show me now your ways, that I may know you in order to find favor in your sight. Consider too that this nation is your people.
> (—Exodus 33:13 ESV)

If we want a greater relationship with God, if we want to be more intimate and deeply acquainted with him, to perceive, recognise, and understand more clearly, we should fast and humble ourselves to have a teachable spirit. Moses was teachable, listened to God, and obeyed God. That we may be acquainted with him, that is the key. What do you want? Can people tell when we have been with the Lord? The Israelites knew Moses had been with God. God wants us to be hungry for more and more of himself. Are you hungry? Do you want more and more and more of God? That's my prayer. Is it yours? I've been praying this, and I've almost said, "Lord, I didn't have any idea that it could involve such pain." The more we surrender, the more he comes.

Moses, a humble man, said, "Show me, teach me Your way, Lord, I want to understand and be acquainted with you more. Lord, that you will be pleased with me." When he recognised he needed God's help, he asked for it. We are to humble ourselves before God.

Psalm 25:4 (ESV), He guides the humble in His ways, (2 Chronicles 7:14). God will teach us his way, and we will walk in his truth. If we spend more time with the Lord in our heart, we will walk in the truth.

Psalm 84:2 (ESV) tells us my soul yearns, even faints for the courts of the Lord. My heart and my flesh cry out for the Living God. If we are not hungry for God, we must make ourselves hungry. If we desire others to move in faith and power, we show this by example. When they see we pray and have answers, that we value the Bible and live by a worldview reflected in the word, they will follow our example. As we behold his glory, his presence changes us into his likeness (2 Corinthians

3:18 ESV). We are to be changing all the time, from glory to glory, in the presence of the Lord.

Exodus 33 14-18 (ESV), Moses said to the Lord, 'If your presence does not go with us, do not carry us up from here. God says to Moses, My presence will go with you and I will give you rest. God said to Moses, I will do the things you ask, because I am pleased with you and I know you by name. For by what shall it be known that I, and your people, have found favor in your sight? Is it not in Your going with us so that we are distinguished, I and Your people, from all the other people upon the face of the earth. I will do this thing also that you have asked, for you have found favor, loving-kindness and mercy in my sight, and I know you personally and by name." (Revelation 2:17 ESV) Moses said, "Show me your glory."

There, on the mountain for six days, he entered the cloud with the Lord for forty days and forty nights, without eating or drinking. God would speak to him face-to-face. Just as he gave Moses a new name, God gives us a new name, which only we and he understand. Yes, he will do the things we ask if we have found favor with him, if he is pleased with us. When God goes with us, it distinguishes us, as we find favor with those to whom we go. God had promised to be with Moses. Without God, we are nothing. I need his presence, don't you? We must not go out without God's presence, as what can we do without God? (Exodus 24:18, 34:28 ESV).

God wants to have greater knowledge of us, then he will answer when we ask. Moses said to God, "Show me Your glory" (Exodus 34:5-10 ESV).

God answered my prayer, which I had prayed for an entire year. "Lord, take me back to Minna Harlem, and please, Lord, let Roberto walk!"

Is God pleased with you? Does he answer your prayers? God's pleasure is clear as he showed Moses his ways and taught him his paths. God credited his faith to him as righteousness. "Without faith it is impossible to please God" (Hebrews 11:6 ESV). All believers appreciate God is God, but many do not understand or perceive him as the rewarder of those who diligently seek him.

> Without faith it is impossible to please Him, for he that cometh to God must believe that He is the rewarder of them that diligently seek Him.
> (—Hebrews 11:6 KJV)

Is he pleased with you? The only thing that makes us different is the Lord. We need God to come. If he doesn't come, we are at our end. Moses said, "Show me your glory." When God shows us the glory, he gets the glory! He wanted more and more of God. We can have many things, but we must want God himself. Many people want power, they want gifts, they want to see God move, but we must want God for who he is and not for what he will do for us! How wonderful to have the manifest presence of God? He will not do it unless we are willing.

He is the rewarder of them who diligently seek him. Because we accept he is the rewarder, we ask him, and we receive. We lift up our hand, and he puts down his hand. We lift our voice; he puts down his voice. We reach towards him; he reaches towards us. There must be a firm foundation; buildings must have deep foundations. Our foundation is to experience God and to have no doubt he rewards those who diligently seek him, to accept he does not lie and that we can trust him to fulfil his word (Psalm 119:160 ESV).

Can people see we differ from others? Moses came to the tent of meeting and could not enter because of the great glory of God. Our relationship with God should reveal the glory of God to others. When Moses came down from the mountain, his face shone with the glory of God. He put a cover over his face as the people could not look upon his face. We can see the glory of God reflected through us because of our relationship with God. God wants us to be starving and radiate his personality (Exodus 34:29-33; 40:34, 35 ESV).

If only God could find one person who could agree to his terms and conditions, there is no limit to what God can do. Wigglesworth spoke with God every fifteen minutes, and every day he celebrated communion, the love feast with the Lord. Wigglesworth met God's conditions. So too did Amy Semple McPherson and Kathryn Kuhlman. What about you? He gets the glory. What about Brother Lawrence in the book *Practising the Presence of God*? He constantly spoke with the Lord.

Moses went up the mountain. God called to him, and he obeyed to spend time with God. Everything he heard from God, he revealed to the people. This led them into a closer relationship with the Lord and brought to them the presence of God. They could be aware and appreciate God, and God could heed them. We must do that. We can go into the presence of God, then go to others and share of our relationship, build them up, and lead them to a closer relationship. Our faith and our obedience come out of our relationship as we pray and spend time with God. When we seek God more, we want more of God, and we hearken him more. Do you hear his voice? Has God spoken to you lately? God spoke often to Moses. God speaks to us through the word. God speaks to us through a gentle whisper as he did to Elijah on the mountain, not in the wind, or storm, or fire, but in a gentle whisper. Sometimes it is just a stirring in our spirit, not a fancy voice, but a sense to do something. When we feel that we must do it as if we ignore it, we can miss God.

One day, as I drove to do some church visitation, I sensed a stirring to visit a particular woman right then. I obeyed that stirring, and that day that woman came to know Jesus Christ as Lord and Savior. Can people tell when we have been with the Lord?

An American preacher would visit Smith Wigglesworth. When he would visit him, he said, "He'd wear me out." I'd walk into his house about ten o'clock in the morning, and he would jump up and down with his arms around me, shouting and praising God. An eighty-year-old man and a twenty-five-year-old man. He had his arms around me, shouting and jumping! Then he would say, "Listen to this," and he would read a chapter from the Bible. When he finished reading, he would say, "Now you need a blessing," and he would lay hands on me and pray for another thirty minutes, and I had not said "good morning" yet. As soon as he got through, he would say, "Oh yes! And here's another scripture you need," and he'd read me another scripture. Then he would say, "Do you have all the gifts of the Holy Spirit?" No, you don't. And he would lay hands on me and pray again. When his daughter called for lunch, she led him to the table. I had become so dizzy and still had not said "good morning"! No wonder he had such a power-filled ministry, he knew God.

> The earnest heart-felt prayer of a righteous man makes tremendous power available, dynamic in its working.
> (—James 5:16 ESV)

God wants to give us more, for he is patient with us and loving. He picks us up when we fall, not just once or twice, but also patiently, again and again, gently nurturing us.

Moses had the obedience of faith (Hebrews 11:23-28 ESV). By faith, Moses's parents were prompted to save him; by faith, Moses aroused to serve God; by faith, he preferred God; by faith, it motivated him to deliver the people, and by faith, he celebrated the Passover in obedience to the word of the Lord.

Hebrews 5:8 says, "Jesus learnt obedience by the things which He suffered," and so did Moses. He had to listen. As do we? When he didn't listen, it cost him dearly (Numbers 20 ESV). He did not speak to the rock but hit it, and as a result, he could not enter the promised land.

Psalm 27 (ESV) has much to say about relationship with the Lord. The psalmist asks God to teach, show, and guide him, and we should do so too. In verse 4, it says, "That we may dwell in the house of the Lord and behold His beauty." When we behold him, it will change us to be like him, as Moses changed. Moses put a cover over his face because the glory of the Lord lit his face and the people could not look upon it, but when he entered the presence of the Lord, he removed the veil (Exodus 34:29-35). Verse 14 tells us we are to wait for the Lord. By faith and prayer, we are to be strong, to take heart, and wait for God.

> Teach me Your way, O Lord, and I will walk and live in Your truth, direct and unite my heart solely and reverently to fear and honour Your name.
> (—Psalm 86:11 ESV)

God will teach us his way, when we trust, lean on, believe in, and commit our all, confidently looking to him, without fear or doubt (Psalm 84:2, 86:2 ESV).

God said to Moses, "There is a place by Me, come and stand in it and I will cause My goodness to pass by before you" (Exodus 33:21-22 ESV). We are to come into that place where we are in the presence of God. We are to come into the secret place of the Most High God to dwell there in that secret place, abiding under His shadow, in that place of protection, where the enemy cannot touch us (Psalm 91:1 ESV).

If we are not hungry for God, we must make ourselves hungry. I have found that rising early in the morning to pray is a key. There are few distractions at 5:00 a.m. The phone does not ring. People do not want to talk to you at 5:00 a.m. (Psalm 42:1-3 ESV). If we are going to move in faith and power, we must pray and read the word. We must do it first because we cannot lead people on further than we have gone ourselves. We need to seek God for who he is, not for what he will do. God wants us to love him with all our heart and soul and mind. He wants all, not 10 per cent, 50 per cent, or 70 per cent, but 100 per cent.

When we behold his glory through spending time with him, God's presence touches and changes us, and we are changing from glory to glory because his presence is in us and on us. Moses brought change because of God's presence with him. We are to go with God's presence. We must not go without it. Remember what Moses said, "If you don't go with me!" What can we do without God?

Psalm 105:4 (TPT) tells us to seek more of his strength! Seek more of him! Let's always be seeking the light of his face. Let's seek and crave his strength, his might and his inflexibility to temptations. Let's seek his face continually.

We can strengthen ourselves in the Lord by talking with God, coming into his presence with praise and worship, praising the name of Jesus and speaking in tongues. When we pray in tongues, we release God's divine secrets for our lives, and we must tap into those secrets. We are to fan into flame the gift of God that is within us (2 Timothy 1:6; 1 Corinthians 14:2 ESV). We are to dig down deep in the word of God to deepen our relationship with the Lord. The Bible speaks of wells, and we can liken these wells to our relationship with the Lord. Have you considered how deep is your well?

Genesis 26:12 (ESV) speaks of Isaac, the son of Abraham, remembered as a man who built wells. What is so significant about wells? When you build a well, you have the right to the water. Everywhere Isaac travelled, he constantly built wells. The Philistines fought over the water of these wells, the key to productivity of the land. Isaac reopened the wells of his father, he remembered, and gave them the same names.

Collins Dictionary definition of *well* is "an underground spring feeds a well, a well is a collection of water deep in the earth."

A well is pure and clear, not muddy or polluted. There is abundant water, water that brings life. We must dig wells in our lives. Ask yourself the following questions: How deep is your well? What kind of well do you have? Where are you digging? What does your well produce? There are two kinds of wells: shallow and deep.

It's superficial, like my story of the pastor and his wife who needed to spend more time with each other and love each other more. Pride, neglect, anger, and jealousy filled their well. When they changed, their well became a deep well of love and trust.

> Out of the overflow of the heart the mouth speaks. By your words you will be acquitted, by your words you will be condemned. Backbiting, resentment, gossip, quarreling, disruption, disharmony, jealousy, are not of God, they come from the flesh, from the pit.
> (—Matthew 12:34 ESV)

> If it's not good and honourable, and of good report, don't say it.
> (—Philippians 4:8 ESV)

A woman who travelled operated out of a shallow well. When she became overtired, she became angry and irrational, full of argument and dissension and strife. She promised much help to brothers in need but never fulfilled her many shallow promises. She had not learnt to put her roots down deep and draw divine strength for her need.

Or a deep well like Paula, who waited, hoped, trusted, believed God all her life for nearly seventy years for fulfilment of a prophetic word over her life. She expected God to do it, even though it had looked hopeless. By faith, she travelled to India. By faith, she expected, without a doubt, that God would use her. There, she became free, delivered from legalistic oppression over her life, and cried when she taught for the first time. A beautiful worshipper, she had a deep well of trust in God.

PAULA

There is the deep well spoken of in Psalm 1 and Jeremiah 17 (ESV). Both passages speak of early in the morning, rising to seek the Lord. When we take the word of God and put it in our heart, supernatural power comes. As we delight in the word of God and in the ways of God, we rely upon the Lord.

Psalm 1:1-3 (ESV) "Blessed is the man who does not walk in the counsel of the wicked or stand in the way of sinners or sit in the seat of mockers." "But his delight (desire) is in the law of the LORD, and on His law (precepts and instructions) he meditates day and night (on the teachings of God). He is like a tree planted by streams of water, which yields its fruit in season and whose leaf does not wither. Whatever he does, prospers."

We are to be like a tree of faith, washed by the water of the word, with our roots planted down deep in that word where we stand and have no doubt in the integrity of the word. There is life-giving wisdom found in the well of God's word.

John 4:14 (ESV) speaks of the woman of Samaria who came to the well, a place of revelation, of the water of life.

We all need revelation from God, the revelation of the spirit in our lives revealing who Jesus really is. We were in a full eight-seater compartment on a Bulgarian train. I nodded to Annie, our interpreter, and shared with a woman sitting there about how God had brought us to Bulgaria. The lady focused and then stated that she lived next door to a Pentecostal church. Right on her wall, she listened to every service, to the worship and every sermon. Her granddaughter attended church regularly. She said, "I know about God, but how do I get to follow him?"

How wonderful for us to reveal to her the way of salvation and to pray the prayer of faith with her. She gave her life to Jesus in that moment. She had no sooner finished praying when the train stopped and she left.

> With joy will you draw water
> from the well of salvation.
> (—Isaiah 12:3 ESV)

What joy that this woman had drawn from the well of salvation and been born again. The well spring of life flowed here, causing us to worship (Genesis 26:23–25 ESV).

Numbers 21:17 (ESV) says of the well of joy, "Spring up O well within my soul." This is the joy God releases. When we dwell in the presence of God, joy is released.

A tough meeting in the middle of the cane fields, in a dark demonic area, unbelievers crowded the tiny church and stood outside.

With a lot of noise and no microphone, the altar call came, and I called for the people to come to Jesus. Four people came forward, among them a tiny child. I reached down to the child, put my hand on her, and said, "A little child shall lead them! Won't you come to Jesus? Please come to Jesus. He gave his life for you."

I pleaded with the people, and suddenly, the platform filled with children. About thirty children were born again that night, and angels rejoiced with great joy in heaven.

Each year I visited this little church, and the next year there were the noisy children in the front rows. As the service progressed, so did the noise. The once full church gradually emptied, and at one stage I looked around as I preached and thought, "Soon I will be the only one left!"

We had the usual call, and all came for prayer. The spirit of the Lord swept over those noisy children, and they were noisy no more. Incredible to see as the entire group were on the floor, laid out flat! A sign and a wonder, so much so that the people poured back into the church and many came to Jesus. What joy this brought to the Father's heart. The pastor, a tiny lady, had a most beautiful experience in which the spirit of the Lord came upon her, and she lay on the floor full of joy, worshipping the Lord, singing to him.

A year later, as I moved towards a leader, he fell sideways with a crash! At first, I thought it to be the spirit of God, but as he manifested on the floor, I quickly realised he had demonic oppression! We prayed and prayed for him, but nothing happened, and the entire church needed prayer. The leadership desperately wanted to see him free, reluctantly stopped praying, as we needed to pray for the others. I asked the people if they wanted the joy of the Lord. They all nodded, and in a group, we asked God to release his joy. We said, "Lord, we receive your joy by faith."

The joy of the Lord came, and the first person to receive this, the young man. He laughed and laughed, in fact, almost paralytic with laughter as she rolled on the floor shrieking, totally set free. The joy of the Lord came! His mother gave him a potion in coffee of ground frogs' sexual parts offered to Satan, and he became demonised when he unknowingly drank the coffee! Praise God for the freedom the joy of the Lord brings. God is full of joy when people are born again of the spirit of the Lord. The angels in heaven rejoice.

Psalm 84:6 (ESV) speaks of the valley of Bacca, a place of springs, a spacious place, a place that brings life.

Song of Solomon 4:15 speaks of a well of fresh water, pure clear, clean, cool, flowing, refreshing water. This was that well.

Isaiah 58:11 (ESV) speaks of a well-watered garden; our lives watered by the word.

There is a well of consecration in 2 Samuel 23:15-17 (ESV), and it speaks of David who poured out the water obtained from the pure clear well at Bethlehem (as an offering to the Lord). He said, "Shall I offer to the Lord that which costs me nothing?"

The king wanted the threshing floor of Araunah the Jebusite. Araunah offered it to him for nothing, and David said, "I will not sacrifice to the Lord my God burnt offerings that cost me nothing" (2 Samuel 24:24 ESV).

He insisted on paying the full price. We must sacrifice everything to the Lord——all our love, all our time, all our money, all our lives——everything! We die to self daily, every day dying as God changes us. More of you and less of us.

Would they offer the Lord what cost them nothing? It cost Mia and Nona all their clothes when the big bag they were sharing for the mountain trip got left behind. When they had to go out and buy a few smalls and share shawls offered by the leader to keep warm. In their room, they used plastic bottles with scalding water to dry smalls. Will we offer the Lord what costs us nothing? When everyone asked to hug the person in the row in front, Mia noticed the woman in front of her entirely filthy, hair, clothes, body! How could she do that? But shall we offer the Lord that which costs us nothing? In obedience to the call, she reached for the woman, hugged her tight, and prayed for God's love to flow! The woman, surprised, responded with tears. The next day the lady, unrecognisable, happily appeared in a clean sari, smelling nice, clean.

NONA AND MIA IN THE MIDDLE
BESIDE JEAN AND PAULA

Lives laid down, we left New Zealand by faith; left behind families and grandchildren with more to come. Yes, it cost us everything—— birthdays, family celebrations, support when our granddaughter was diagnosed with leukemia and our son-in-law with cancer, spending time with old friends, even losing contact with friends. Shall we offer the Lord that which costs us nothing? No. We give all. What couple at our ages leaves their home, country, friends, family to travel with $800 to unknown places? What couple at our ages travels the world, with hours on planes, to filthy places, stays in grimy hotels on thin hard beds? It's costly to follow Jesus to lay down our rights——rights to a pleasant house, a car or cars; right to retire; right to a lifestyle in beautiful New Zealand surrounded by excellent food and beautiful beaches, surrounded by family and friends. Yes, shall we offer to the Lord that which costs us nothing? We have given all for over thirty years.

We were in a new three-month-old house church. They crowded the little house with about thirty people. We had prayed for all, and God had moved in substantial power. Almost as an after-thought, I felt to ask the people, "Have you given your lives to Jesus?"

Amazed, I discovered that more than half the people in the room wanted to be born again! What a privilege to lead them all to Jesus. The greatest miracle of all is when people come to Jesus and give their lives to him.

> Have Your own way, Lord, Have Your own way, You are the potter; I am the clay. Mold me and make me after Your will, While I am waiting, yielded and still.
> —George Stebbins, 1907

We are to follow on to know the Lord. We can know about him, but we need to know him. When we seek him, he will come to us and change us.

SUPPLEMENTARY QUESTIONS TO CHALLENGE AND INSPIRE

How can you increase your hunger for God?

What were the keys in Moses's life that caused God to call him "My friend?"

How can we find favor with God?

Passion, intimacy, and love are keywords in a relationship. Look again at the meanings of these words and test how you can increase each of the factors in your relationship with Jesus.

THE HOW-TO OF CHANGING UP A GEAR, RELEASING VISION

FAITH AND OBEDIENCE AND RELATIONSHIP RELEASE VISION

At the close of 1990, I prayed, "Lord, take me to Asia," as I believed that I would go for an extended period to visit Myanmar with Bibles, to do medical work in Thailand, and travel to China. I suffered terribly with a painful hip. I had visited the specialist, and the cause appeared unexplainable! The pain, so bad, I had to lift my leg physically to walk up steps, and I avoided walking. When I asked for ministry at a Rise-Up Rally, they brought a prophetic word over my life, that God had called me to the four corners of the earth, and that Satan tried to cripple me. The trip I had been on a few months earlier only began what God wanted to do.

Stunned, I returned home to look at a map. When I did, I saw Russia at the top of the world, and I said, "Lord, am I going to go there?"

I studied the map and saw on one side the Middle East and on the other side Cuba. I said, "God, I don't really want to go there."

New Zealand is at the bottom of the world, and I said, "Lord, you can to do it because if you are calling me to these places, it has to be you that does it."

Back in 1990, in New Zealand, difficulties for women in ministry persisted. I fasted and prayed that God would cause it to happen. I spoke it into being. "Lord, I will go to Cuba, I will go to Russia, I will go to the Middle East, and I will minister throughout New Zealand in the name of Jesus."

Every day I spoke prophetically over the world map as I spoke the vision into being by faith.

The problem with my hip remained. I stood on the word, proclaiming it daily over my life, that the name of Jesus healed me. I had no freedom from pain until I embarked on the plane to Asia many months later!

The night before that trip started, our landlord called to say he wanted to talk to Kevin about the rent. We were concerned, thinking he would want to lift the rent; we were already paying $160 a week, a lot for that time! But when Kevin spoke with him, it amazed him. Not only did he reduce our rent to $120 a week, but it also remained at that price for the next six years! Our God is the God of miracles who act on behalf of those who wait on him.

Vine's dictionary says, "Vision is to behold; divine revelation; This is a means by which God communicates divine messages; the act of seeing; of coming into view.

Easton's dictionary says, "Vision is an experience in the life of a person, and they receive a special revelation from God."

The revelation from God had two purposes. First, God gave a vision for immediate direction: as with Abram in Genesis 12:1-3 (ESV), as with Lot in Genesis 19:15 (ESV), as with Balaam in Numbers 22:22-40

(ESV), and as with Peter in Acts 12:7 (ESV). Second, a vision came to develop the kingdom of God. It can reveal the moral and spiritual deficiencies of the people of God. Vision reflects God's requirements to maintain a proper relationship with him. The vision of prophets, namely Isaiah, Amos, Hosea, Micah, Ezekiel, Daniel, and John, are representative of this aspect of revelation.

Negatives in films are just negative until we develop them. With a 35 mm camera with a film, if you take a photo, it's not a photo until you develop it. It's the same with vision, the call of God, guidance; the Bible says much about vision.

Proverbs 29:18 (ESV) says, "Without a vision, the people perish." That means us as Christians, as vision comes from the word of God.

Where there is no vision, no redemptive revelations of God, the people perish, they cast off restraint, and they are disorderly. It makes them naked; it scatters the people, the ruin of the land comes.

Collins says, "Restraint is the ability to control, to moderate impulses, passions. The opposite of restraint is disorderly, unruly, untidy, irregular and uncontrolled."

Imagine God sees us as naked when there is no vision and, worse, disorderly and without restraint! It's as though we are standing on a rotten log!

> And the LORD answered me: "Write the vision; make it plain on tablets, so he may run who reads it. For still the vision awaits its appointed time; it hastens to the end—it will not lie. If it seems slow, wait for it; it will surely come; it will not delay.
> (—Habakkuk 2:2-3 ESV)

That everyone who passes by may be able to read it easily and quickly as he hastens by. The vision is for a special time, and it speeds to its fulfilment; it will not deceive or disappoint. Wait for it earnestly because it will surely come.

Write the vision, write the revelation, make it plain. It waits for the right time; don't get impatient.

Vision is not by chance; it is a choice. We choose to move into the direction God is leading us. We must receive a clear vision of where we are going. Abraham had a glorious vision.

> The Lord had said to Abram, "Leave your country, your people and your father's household and go to the land I will show you. I will make you into a great nation and I will bless you; I will make your name great, and you will be a blessing. I will bless those who bless you, and whoever curses you, I will curse; and all peoples on earth will be blessed through you." So Abram left, as the lord had told him; and Lot went with him. Abram was seventy-five years old when he set out from Haran. He took his wife Sarai, his nephew Lot, all the possessions they had accumulated and the people they had acquired in Haran, and they set out for the land of Canaan, and they arrived there. Abram travelled through the land as far as the site of the great tree of Moreh at Shechem. At that time the Canaanites were in the land. The lord appeared to Abram and said, "To your offspring I will give this land." So he built an altar there to the Lord.
> (—Genesis 12:1-7 ESV)

> The Lord said to Abram after Lot had parted from him, "Lift up your eyes from where you are and look north and south, east and west. All the land

> that you see I will give to you and your offspring forever. I will make your offspring like the dust of the earth, so that if anyone could count the dust, then your offspring could be counted. Go, walk through the length and breadth of the land, for I am giving it to you. Arise, walk about the land through its length and breadth; for I will give it to you."
> (—Genesis 13:14-17 ESV)

Yes, God said to Abraham, "Leave your country and go! Lift your eyes and I will give you all you behold." On that trip to Asia in 1990, I had a tremendous sense that God said this to me. Abraham had a choice. It's a choice to move, as God won't force us. We choose to walk and take the land. Before I left New Zealand, I arranged to visit a boy we had sponsored for several years with World Vision in North Thailand, on instructions from World Vision. The instructions said go to Phayao and stay at the Cham Kham Hotel. At eight in the morning, a person from World Vision would come and take me to the project village.

I obeyed and travelled to Phayao but, very disturbed, found this to not be a city but an entire district! I stayed overnight in a hotel where no one spoke English, daunting on my first trip alone! On the bus that evening to Phayao, I sat with a girl who spoke English. She became concerned to discover I travelled not knowing where and at night alone! I had no fear as God had spoken that he would go with me, that he would go before. Every place I travelled would be mine! She kindly made enquiries to find that a bus that travelled to a place called Cham Kham near the Laos border at six o'clock the next morning. I journeyed for two hours on the rickety old bus, arriving in the dusty village of Cham Kham at 8:00 a.m. On arrival, I climbed on a rickshaw and just around the corner, above a building, a sign read, Cham Kham Hotel! I praised God that he had brought me that far by his grace, that he had led me there. At 8:30 a.m., a woman from World Vision took me to the project to meet Sonjan. That day I identified with Abraham who left by faith, not knowing where he would go.

Ecclesiastes 5:1, 3, 7 (ESV) tells us to keep your foot, give your mind to what you are doing when you go, for to draw near to hear and obey is better than to give the sacrifice of fools. Much dreaming and many words are useless, for a dream comes with much busyness and painful effort. In a multitude of dreams, there is futility and worthlessness; there must be more than just dreaming.

God lays out a plan, and we must walk in it (Ephesians 2:10 ESV).

Abraham had a vision to take the land. Do we possess a vision to take our nation for Jesus? Joshua took the land by faith and moved without doubt. We are to move into villages, towns, cities, and nations by faith.

Nothing is impossible to God. Our God delights to do the impossible. How often do we consider this? Without a vision, the people perish. People are going to hell because we do not reach them. All outstanding leaders possess two things: they know where they are going, and they can get people to follow them. Are others catching your vision? Are you leading them? People rise to vision. If you operate with no vision, you will lead no one. Abraham acted full of vision and faith. Noah built a boat in faith and vision, in an area with no water, and he did not even know about rain! He looked stupid. He took 120 years to make this boat. Imagine the ridicule he faced, this man of faith, of vision. Reader, are you a man, a woman of vision? Vision is the foundation to witness in God what it can be and will be. We must move forward in faith. When you change gear, you move through the gears by faith, you expect that gear to change, you expect to move forward when you speed up; vision is like that. Vision is the foundation to what we will become tomorrow and in the future. Vision makes us a bigger person in God. We must master where we are at before we move on. We must be faithful with what we possess (Luke 16:10, Matthew 25:21 ESV).

One who is faithful in a very little is also faithful in much, and one who is dishonest in a very little is also dishonest in much. If then you have not

> been faithful in the unrighteous wealth, who will entrust to you the true riches? And if you have not been faithful in that which is another's, who will give you that which is your own?
> (—Luke 16:10-12 ESV)

If we yield to faithfulness, this will become predominant in our lives. We are to be honest. We are to be faithful and walk in love. Faithfulness brings increase. We need to say, "Thank you, Lord, for my job, my home, my husband, my family. I'm going to be the best I can be." We are to sow and do whatever we do unto the Lord.

Let us look at Judges 6, at the life of Gideon. Gideon, a man of faith and vision, had a heart to raise the purpose of God, but he did not start that way.

> The angel of the LORD came and sat down under the oak in Ophrah that belonged to Joash the Abiezrite, where his son Gideon threshed wheat in a winepress to keep it from the Midianites. When the angel of the LORD appeared to Gideon, he said, "The LORD is with you, mighty warrior." "But, sir," Gideon replied, "if the LORD is with us, why has all this happened to us? Where are all his wonders that our fathers told us about when they said, did not the LORD bring us up out of Egypt? But now the LORD has abandoned us and put us into the hand of Midian." The LORD turned to him and said, "Go in the strength you possess and save Israel out of Midian's hand. Am I not sending you?" "But, LORD," Gideon asked, "how can I save Israel? My clan is the weakest in Manasseh, and I am the least in my family." The LORD answered, "I will be with you, and you will strike down all the Midianites together."
> (—Judges 6:11-16 ESV)

Here is Gideon, trusted with what he had, faithful; he worked in the winepress. There, in that dusty, dirty place, he threshed wheat. I don't know if you have ever seen wheat threshed, but we were in Nepal for the rice harvest. On the roofs of the houses, across from where we stayed, there were women threshing rice. As it raised great dust, when they beat the grain, the ladies wore cloths around their faces, and the wind took the chaff away. They were in a prominent place to do this task. Gideon hid low down, in a wine press from the Midianites who oppressed his people. When they observed dust rising from the threshing, they rode across the valley and stole the wheat. These Midianites had oppressed the people of Israel for seven years because of their idolatry (Judges 6:1 ESV). And the angel of the LORD appeared to him and said to him, "The LORD is with you, O mighty man of valour." The angel of the Lord came and sat under an oak tree beside where Gideon was in the winepress. This angel had a message for Gideon. I assume he had never seen an angel before, so what would be his reaction? I assume he experienced terror! This message seemed to cause even greater terror, as the angel said, "The Lord is with you, you are a mighty man of fearless courage." Other translations say, "mighty man of valour," "mighty warrior," "valiant warrior." That is how God beheld him. He didn't regard himself that way as he was frightened, scared. His reply reveals how he regarded himself and his situation: If the Lord is with us, why has all this happened to us? Where are all the wonders that our fathers told us about? Why has God forsaken us? These were not words of faith and vision. These were words of doubt and unbelief! He questioned God. Gideon did not realise the problems resulted from the people's sin. We must be careful to acknowledge God's faithfulness. We should not blame God in adverse circumstances.

What is our reply when God speaks to us? Do we question God? We are to start seeing as God sees, from God's perspective. Revelation and vision are the superimposition of God's plan over our natural circumstances.

In my dream, my finger moved around the coast of Turkey and up around a country beside Turkey, and I heard a voice, "Bulgaria!" Three days later, a woman in a church spoke to me in English from Bulgaria!

This happened in Cuba! Later that week, some pastors were praying with me about my dream. They prophesied that one day I would surely go to Bulgaria and God would move in power and might, as he did in Cuba. Two years later, before I visited Bulgaria, I met the woman again unexpectedly in a different Cuban city, and she gave me the name of her pastor in Sofia, Bulgaria, who opened doors for me in that nation!

Elizabeth, who travelled with me in 1998 to Bulgaria and Russia, had a dream that a young woman appeared to her, pleading with her to come over and help us. As a result, when my newsletter arrived at her house two days later, she responded and came on the trip.

BULGARIA DENISE FANNY AND ELISABETH

Dreams and visions speed up gear change to God's revelation. We should test and confirm any sense of divine leading that we receive.

Verse 12 tells us that God knew Gideon's potential. God regarded Gideon as a mighty warrior, fearless; entirely against the natural. In the natural Gideon, a timid, frightened man hid. We are to call forth what is possible in God, declare ourselves as God sees us. God says we can do anything in the name of Jesus.

Vision is the substance of outstanding achievement. God chooses the weak to confound the wise (1 Corinthians 1:27 ESV). God chooses weak people. He raised up this weak man. Promotion comes from God.

Gideon didn't say, "Hey, God! I'm glad you spoke." Gideon argued! Can you identify with Gideon? Would you ever argue with God? God spoke to him three times, and Gideon said, "But God!" Imagine saying "but" to God and being full of excuses. Twice, he said, "I can't." When we say, "I can't," God says, "I can." God reveals, but we must seek the revelation. By faith, we look at what it can be, will be, but God sees the final completed picture. What is our answer to the Lord? Do we say, "Yes, Lord" or "But?" In verse 16, the Lord says, "I will be with you." Twice, God says this to Gideon, "Go and I will be with you." He doesn't ask us to do it on our own. He says he will go with us. Remember the words of Jesus, "I am with you, I will never leave you or forsake you" (Matthew 28:20 ESV). He does not ask us to do the impossible. He does that. He asks us to do what is possible, and he does the rest.

When I visited Asia in 1990, God said he would be with me, and I would never be alone. And never in the six weeks did I feel lonely or alone, as I always felt God with me. God said, "Go in the strength you received." God recognised Gideon's strength. Gideon believed he had no strength. Gideon said, "I am the weakest, I am the least, I am the poorest in my family." He questioned God!

Do we do that? We are to confess our situation as God sees it, not as it appears. We are not to look at the circumstances but at God who is greater than the circumstances. God commissioned Gideon to save the people out of Midian's hand. To Gideon, this appeared nothing short of ridiculous, as only a few minutes earlier, he had been hiding from the Midianites. And God told him to save Israel!

God's reply, "I will be with you, you will strike down all the Midianites as one man" (Judges 6:16). When we go, we go in God's strength, not our own. We are to believe God strengthens those he calls and commissions and trust in the promise of his abiding presence (Judges 6:14-16 ESV). Gideon said, "If I have found favor in Your eyes, give me a sign" (Judges 6:17 ESV). Still, Gideon wanted confirmation. Though Gideon beheld the angel, he still asked God for a sign. Could this be frank unbelief? Do we do this? Do we receive a revelation and ask God to confirm it? Why does he need to? Many people hear from God and then ask God for more confirmation. Sometimes we need to just do it.

A woman visited her pastor and asked, "I want you to pray with me about going with Denise to Myanmar."

He replied, "Just do it. You've had buckets of prayer and need no more, just get up and do it!"

What are you waiting for—lightening in the sky? Let me encourage you—just do it! Just do it! That's my story—just do it!

Just do it! Many people receive prophecies, dreams, and visions and write them in a book or even several books. They say I received these wonderful words from God, but when you ask them what they are doing about them, they say, "I'm waiting for them to happen. I'm waiting for God to show me more and do it!" That is operating on a red light, the light of stop and even reverse, taking us backwards. There is no forward motion!

I want to challenge you if you are like this. Rise. Take the books, the words. Speak them into being, and do something about them. Otherwise, they will never happen. The time is too short. Jesus is coming back for a church that is doing the works and living the life, not waiting for some miracle to happen, but making it happen! God will not pull your feet out of the concrete. *You just have to do it!*

Remember God said, "Don't be afraid!" Fear not, don't be afraid. It is repeated over three hundred times! We must develop a clear vision of the next level God is taking us to. Every new level we come to is a battle with new devils! Vision leads us into our inheritance.

> The Lord came to Gideon and said, Take the second cow from your father's herd, tear down your father's altar to Baal and cut down the Asherah pole beside it. (—Judges 6:25 ESV)

The angel instructed him to build an altar to the Lord and use the wood from the Asherah pole, sacrifice the bull as a burnt offering. Gideon obeyed the Lord. He did not argue this time. He did what God said. He broke down the altar, not in the daytime, but secretly at night so that no one would know! Consider this: They must have heard the noise of the animal sacrifice and the pole being chopped down. It's hard, isn't it, to keep a secret when several people are involved. Someone will tell!

We don't just change our perspective, but we must also change our behavior. Gideon changed his behavior. God wants all—he wants everything! Gideon had to turn his faith into action. He had to start with what he had. He had to confront fear of failure, fear of man, and idolatry. We must look at ourselves and deal with the issues in our lives in these areas. Gideon's faith had risen. He looked beyond the trials and obstacles to know that God is sovereign over such and used them to shape and strengthen himself for future battles. His faith had to rely on God, ever-present, to bring the answers and supply his present need.

Yet there is opposition for trials to build character. We must persevere and not give up. They wanted to kill Gideon. He had become unpopular. They killed Jesus and the apostles! There is a price to pay for the plan and purpose of God. Do not think it will be easy! We build great destiny on noble character.

Do you consider it to be easy when we left New Zealand with $800? Of course not! He never asks us to do what is easy. He asks us to do the impossible as he is our God. If it's impossible, he knows we need his help to achieve it! When we have a destiny, we need to cut down the difficulties to make it possible. God's vision makes the impossible possible.

God takes the insignificant to do amazing things (Judges 7:2 ESV).

> If you have raced with men on foot and they have worn you out, how can you compete with horses? If you stumble in safe country, how will you manage in the thickets of the Jordan?
> (—Jeremiah 12:5 ESV)

If we are tired of running with men, how will we compete with horses? If you think it has been difficult already, remember there is more to come. Gideon could not rely on his fleshly resources and ability. Gideon had to learn to rely on God's wisdom and power. As he faced an impossible situation, God received all the glory. Now it became even more impossible! God now reduced the number of the Israelite army from thirty-two thousand to three hundred! How would you feel? The Midianites were stretched out across the valley of Jezreel. The odds were bad with thirty-two thousand, but now, except for God, victory seemed impossible! They outnumbered the Israelites. Don't think because you received a vision it will be possible to achieve it. If the vision is of God, there will be aspects of its achievement, which will be impossible!

> It's not by might, nor by power, but by My Spirit," says the Lord.
> (—Zechariah 4:6 ESV)

Obedience to revelation releases power. Authority and leadership come from vision. People gather to the vision. The Holy Spirit anointing makes the impossible possible.

> The Spirit of the Lord came upon Gideon.
> (—Judges 6:34 ESV)

The spirit of the Lord clothed Gideon with himself and took possession of him. Judges 7:11 (ESV) says Gideon listened carefully to the Lord and carefully did what he said. Gideon had to trust God's presence and divine resources rather than his own. Although he did not recognise he had talents and abilities, the spirit of God energised him to see fruit for God. What about us? Isn't this the same for us? To bear fruit for God, the Holy Spirit must energise us.

But he had the dream where a loaf of bread rolled into the enemy camp, just as Gideon arrived to hear the interpretation. But it was an inferior barley loaf, as wheat is the better grain. It meant Israel the lesser and inferior, the Midianites greater and superior, but Israel would be superior! God recognised Gideon's need for courage (Judges 7:11 ESV). God's timing is perfect. God is amazing! Imagine, he had Gideon right there at the very moment the man told his dream!

We must inspire others to follow us. It inspired the people to follow and obey Gideon. They rose to his vision with unity. Good leadership is a key to the triumph of God's purposes. These followers of Gideon led restrained lives, guided by Godly wisdom and God's word. This is an impossible battle as they had no swords with which to defend themselves. Imagine going to war with only jars and torches! In the natural, that is all they had, but in the spiritual, they had the power of God! What more did they need? Gideon knew how to apply what he knew to be true. Gideon determined the Lord's direction and leading for his life and acted on it. We base victory in a situation on what God says and doing what God says. We soak ourselves in the word, and gradually, a new image comes forth in our lives.

There are different levels to vision: There is the person who wanders like a blind person, wandering aimless, happy with a little of God. Then the ones who receive the vision but never enter, happy to be followers. There are only a few who see the vision, move into it, achievers, doers running in the race. Changes gear and moves forward with determination and purpose.

ACTIONS OF PEOPLE OF VISION

Write the vision down and read it regularly. Pray over it. Speak it into being. Call it forth. Surround yourself with people of like vision. It connects vision to people who need to read your vision. A word of advice to the unmarried—don't marry someone who doesn't share your vision. Check them out first. It's important who is in your life. People need to know where you are going to follow you. We must change to adapt to the vision. Be single-minded. Things fail because of divided vision. We are not to be divided but focused. We are to keep on refocusing our vision (Philippians 3:7), putting our trust and hope in Christ alone. People of vision can't waste time. People and things come to steal our vision. We have to take extreme care of our time (Proverbs 14:7 ESV).

Eagles fly alone and are found one at a time.

Vision will do several things for us. Vision stops us going the wrong way and arrests us so we not only accept our position, but also our potential. There are no limits; we are to rise to the possibilities. Vision encourages us to give up all we are for what we will become. When vision gives us an assignment to fulfil, we affect, inspire, and help those around us. Though vision will never be successful until achieved, it will make us excited to say we can do it and we love it. Vision will impel us to perceive others and motivate them to rise and move on. Vision will strengthen us in hard times (Acts 20:22-24). While vision is not a vision until it includes other people, vision is a bridge to help someone else. Vision must become a way of life for us.

Matthew 28:18 (ESV) tell us that "all authority has been given us in heaven and in earth" to go and preach the gospel to all nations. This is a command; we must make disciples and train them to do the same, but we must accept Jesus gave us the power to do this. The precious Holy Spirit gives us this power.

> He said to them, Go into all the world and preach the good news to all creation. Whosoever believes and is baptised will be saved, but whoever does not believe will be condemned. And these signs will accompany those who believe. In My name they will drive out demons, they will speak in new tongues; they will pick up snakes with their hands, and when they drink deadly poison, it will not hurt them at all; they will place their hands on sick people and they will get well.
> (—Mark 16:15-20 ESV)

> You did not choose me, but I chose you and appointed you that you should go and bear fruit and that your fruit should abide, so that whatever you ask the Father in my name, he may give it to you.
> (—John 15:16 ESV)

> Whatever you ask in my name, this I will do, that the Father may be glorified in the Son.
> (—John 14:13)

"Truly, truly, I say to you, whoever believes in me will also do the works that I do; and greater works than these will he do, because I am going to the Father.

Whatever you ask in my name, this I will do, that the Father may be glorified in the Son.

If you ask me anything in my name, I will do it.

God will answer our prayer if we bring forth fruit (John 14:12-13 ESV).

If we are to do the works, greater works, that Jesus did, we must have the power to do the works; the same power that Jesus had is available to you and me. How can we do greater works than Jesus did without the same or greater power? We are to present all that Jesus is to God so that God will grant our requests.

Mani and Julie, pastors in a beautiful beach resort in NZ, obeyed God. Because of their vision to love and serve people, they came several times to Myanmar. There, they encountered a whole new world and had an instant love relationship with the family they met. In this new world, they met new friends, namely Lahtoi and Grace, who made an impact to their lives, as they were filled with humility and love for God.

"I loved the way God used them, their vision and faithfulness. It was life-changing for me," Mani said. "We travelled two hours to the jungle from where we stayed and stopped at this place not far from a pig farm. The smell was bad. A minibus took us in the heavy rain, but what a wonderful presence of God. About 150 believers came. When the people danced, the platform was like a trampoline and was covered with old congoleum. When we saw the great big woks with all the food, we asked, what is all this food for? Surely not for us as we don't need it!"

"For the people," they said. "Some of them have walked two hours to these meetings and need lots of food We were astounded that they would walk two hours just to hear us! In the front of the meeting were all these young women feeding their babies. The presence of God was so amazing, we could never forget it."

Loving the people, they came, although their feet swelled so badly, they could not even put shoes on. They believed, obeyed, and saw God do amazing things. As a result, their love for the family in Myanmar birthed a vision to help the children. For years, they continued to support and still support the work there.

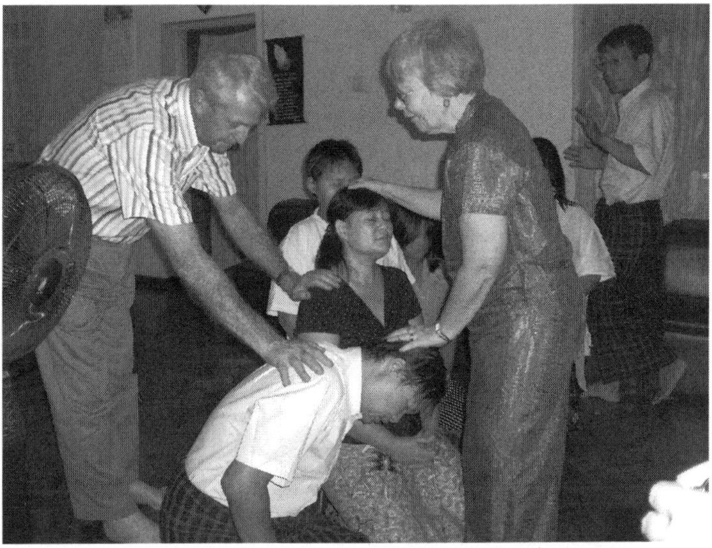

MANI PRAYING FOR PASTOR U ZIN HLA

JULIE AND MANI BESIDE ELISABETH

> You are all sons of God through faith in Christ Jesus. For all of you who were baptised into Christ have clothed yourselves with Christ. There is neither Jew nor Greek, slave nor free, male nor female, for you are all one in Christ Jesus. If you belong to Christ, then you are Abraham's seed, and heirs according to the promise. What I am saying is that as long as the heir is a child, he does not differ from a slave, although he owns the entire estate. He is subject to guardians and trustees until the time set by his father. So also, when we were children, we were in slavery under the basic principles of the world. But when the time had fully come, God sent his Son, born of a woman, born under law, to redeem those under law, that we might receive the full rights of sons. Because you are sons, God sent the Spirit of His Son into our hearts, the Spirit who calls out, "Abba, Father. So you are no longer a slave, but a son; and since you are a son, God has made you also an heir."
> (—Galatians 3:26-4:7 ESV)

We are heirs of God and joint heirs with Christ because God has adopted us as his very own. When we were born again, Jesus came to live in our lives. We are flesh of his flesh and bone of his bone. Believe it! Everything Jesus is and was became ours! As we are not slaves, but sons and daughters of the Living God, we belong to Christ. We are Abraham's seed. The promises of God to Abraham are ours; we are children of Abraham, heirs according to the promise. Jesus came to break the bondage of sin that we might receive the adoption of sons, an heir of God through the Anointed One, reborn into his image. He gives all his power to us. We have a covenant when we are born of God. God sent the spirit of his Son into our hearts (2 Corinthians 1:22; Ephesians 1:13-14 ESV). Every father's desire is to reproduce himself in his son. Every mother's desire is to reproduce herself in her daughter.

The Father's desire is to reproduce himself in us. We are his creation; the life of Jesus is in us.

> My little children, of whom I am again in the pains of childbirth until it forms Christ in you.
> (—Galatians 4:19 ESV)

Christ is to be formed in us. Jesus, the Son of God, the Anointed One, is to be formed in us. The qualities of Jesus are to be qualities of our lives. Some of these qualities are authority, power, boldness, love, and compassion.

In Mark 1:40 (ESV), Jesus took authority over disease. The leper came to Jesus and said to him, "If you are willing, you can make me clean."

Jesus was filled with compassion. He reached out his hand. The man became clean and healed. We take authority over disease and sickness. Disease means dis-ease. People are not at ease when they are sick.

A lady who had undergone surgery for cancer came when she could to the monthly healing service we held. That day the district nurse had been to dress the radiation burns on her surgical scars. These burns were very smelly, painful, and not healing. We prayed for her. Two days later, when the nurse returned to uncover the wounds to dress, the burns were entirely healed.

We had taken authority over cancer and sickness, telling them to go in the name of Jesus. God moved and healed her because he is the Lord, and he does not change (Malachi 3:6). Jesus's power is the same today, and his power flows through you and me.

Mark 4:35 (ESV) tells us that Jesus took authority over the elements. Jesus spoke to the storm, and it stopped. The disciples had the same power. They could have risen and pulled down the anointing and broken the curse over the weather because we can take authority over the conditions. The same power Jesus had, we possess because we are heirs of the Father, joint heirs with the Son. All that the Father is and was comes to us. Jesus, the Son, is heir of all things (Hebrews 1:2 ESV). God appointed him as heir and lawful owner of all things. When we are born again, we inherit this. All power, all authority, all boldness is his, and because it is his, it is ours—yours and mine! We need to comprehend this because when we do, it will transform our lives. For too long, Satan has robbed us of this inheritance.

We can take authority over the elements. There were four of us, and we were in a car going to Guantanamo in Cuba, a three-hour journey from where we had been ministering. I said to the driver, "Do you have enough petrol?"

He shook his head and replied, "No!"

I asked, "Do we need to buy some?"

"No!" he said again. "We will stop the car and pray."

I said, "But look, here are American dollars, and we will give you the money to get the petrol."

"No!" he said. "We cannot waste your precious money on petrol. The church needs the money, not the government. Anyway, there is no petrol here to buy."

I asked, "How much petrol do we have?"

He said, "Only enough for one hour of the journey, and I must return immediately after taking you there!"

We stopped the car and prayed. Fervent prayer rose from that car; we were Western women, not used to travelling with no petrol! After travelling for one hour-thirty, Hosea said, "Praise God, God is multiplying the petrol, only a third is used!"

Yes, we reached Guantanamo. The pastor there gave Hosea a tiny amount of petrol, just enough to get him home, after his petrol finished just 18 km from where we started the journey! Four hours' travel by the grace of God!

Mark 5:1 (ESV) tells us that Jesus took authority over the demons. Like Jesus, we can take authority over the demons.

On trip two to Russia, people coughed and choked and scream whenever I approached them. The demons had to flee at the presence of God. When we walk in a vision, the Holy Spirit is with us wherever we go.

In Cuba Pastor Alipio, a tremendous man of faith and vision, shared a life event. He did not understand the joy that people across the world were experiencing. He had an experience with Satan and God during a ministry trip to the United States. In bed, sleeping, Satan appeared in his room. He laughed and laughed and laughed until he fell out of bed and woke the family with whom he stayed. They gathered outside his room concerned, as it seemed he had gone crazy. When he "came to" after several hours of laughter, the devil had fled, and it changed him. I discovered when this joy of the Lord comes; if the person has demons, the demons flee, and it sets the person free. It is very wonderful. We are carriers of the presence of God.

PASTOR ALIPIO AND OLGA

One day in Cuba, they invited me to go with the pastor's wife to visit a family. This, we did, and while there, busy speaking with a visitor in the home, a professor of English, I noticed in the room's corner sat a coffee table with a large glass plate sitting under a big bowl containing sand. Then there was a sound of a loud bang, as if a gun had gone off. This is not unusual in Cuba, but everyone rushed to the door and looked out on the street. But nothing had happened out there! Amazed, it appeared that glass flew throughout the room and we noticed the glass plate under the bowl had vanished! The man said to me, "What do you make of that?"

I replied, "Witchcraft!"

Louisa, the pastor's wife, nodded and said, "That is why I brought you here—glass tables crack and handles fall off the cups."

I suggested we return the following day with the pastor and the other ladies travelling with me.

On the next day, we returned to pray through this demonised house. The woman had found in the roof some idols and satanic objects, which she had thrown in the river. Yet the week before our arrival in the town, the problems had started. Each room had problems that we dealt with as we prayed and spoke the name of Jesus and the blood of Jesus. Finally, after anointing the walls, doors, and floors with oil, we came to the dark back courtyard. We were all praying when a family member came anxious to tell us that the kitchen table had cracked further! Back we filed into the kitchen, where we stood around the table. Sure enough, it had new cracks! At this point, I became angry with Satan, raised my hands in the air, and brought them down heavily on the table! I shouted, "IN THE NAME OF JESUS!"

As my hands hit the table, we heard a resounding crash as the glass cracked and shattered and the demons fled! The house was now free. We advised this family to pray out loud, read the Bible out loud, and sing Christian songs in the house to keep it free. Yes, at the name of Jesus, demons flee. Remember, though, the demons will not listen to us if we do not have a relationship with God. Change gear, move in vision, and take your God-given authority.

THE WITCHCRAFT HOUSE

Mark 5:21 (ESV) tells us that Jesus took authority over death, over sickness. He brought heaven to earth. When he said the kingdom of heaven is here, the kingdom of heaven is amongst us. He brought heaven to earth. There is no sickness in heaven; sickness had to go wherever he travelled. He raised Jairus's daughter from the dead, healed and raised Lazarus from the dead (John 11). Sickness and death go at the name of Jesus because no sickness or death are in heaven. Jesus had commitment, perseverance, obedience, and submission. God listened to Jesus because of his obedient submission (Hebrews 5:8 ESV).

"As a son, he learnt obedience through the things he suffered." Because he recognised his identity, he stated his inheritance (John 4:26, 6:35 ESV). He knew who he was. He did not turn from his destiny (Hebrews 10:7 ESV).

John 6:35-38 (ESV) tells us that all that the Father has Jesus has, and we are his heirs!

James 2:5 (ESV) says we are to be rich in faith, and as heirs, we are to inherit the kingdom.

In 2 Corinthians 4:13 (ESV), it is said that we have the same spirit of faith that Jesus has because we became a new creation when we were born again.

James 2:17-18 (ESV) tells us that we are to show our faith by our works. How can we show our faith if we show no works?

It is easy to get caught up in our vision and not spend time with the one who gave the vision. Without vision, we show nothing as we are a people who are purposeless. Often there is a division or two visions! This will not bring the blessing of God. We must agree with God and speak the vision into being by faith.

If there is a partner in our lives, the vision must be a unified vision, or there will be division. This vision must drive us into the plan of God. When a couple receive two different visions, there will be no provision as they are operating outside the laws of God

Amos 3:3 (ESV) asks, do two walk together? Unless they have agreed to meet, this gives the suggestion that we have to make an appointment to agree.

A husband and wife need to make an appointment to agree, and make the two visions one vision. To do this, there is a need for harmony and agreement. Many people do not realise there is a lack of results with two visions. Vision comes from the word of God, The meaning of the word "division" is two visions. The key is to communicate, as one vision brings provision. God foresees your need and prepares then provides. God presents the provision.

> We run lawlessly, he that keeps the law will be happy, happy is he.
> (—Proverbs 28:7 ESV)

We must operate between and within God's laws and expect, when we do, that we will have positive expectations and positive results.

> On one occasion, while he was eating with them, He gave them this command: "Do not leave Jerusalem, but wait for the gift My Father promised, which you have heard Me speak about. But you will receive power when the Holy Spirit comes on you; and you will be My witnesses in Jerusalem, and in all Judea and Samaria, and to the ends of the earth."
> (—Acts 1:4-8 ESV)

Things God tells us to do are things we want but will not receive unless we do it!

It says in 1 Corinthians 9:24-27 (ESV), do you not know that in a race, all the runners run, but only one receives the prize? So run that you may obtain it.

Every athlete exercises self-control in all things. They do it to receive a perishable wreath, but we are imperishable.

So I do not run aimlessly. I do not box as one beating the air.

But I discipline my body and keep it under control, lest after preaching to others, I myself should be disqualified.

Many people receive words, dreams, visions from God, but few achieved and realise them. "We are to make the prize ours."

Every athlete goes into strict training, conducts and restricts himself/herself in all things! God wants all! Not 50 per cent, not 60 per cent, but 100 per cent.

> All to Jesus, I surrender. All to him, I freely give. It's easy to sing the song, but we are to run the race!

Relationship with the Lord brings vision and direction, for vision takes courage and perseverance. Vision releases faith, and faith releases obedience. Obedience releases commitment. We need one gear to move into another! Many people receive vision, but few people see the vision realised. Many people are waiting for God to do it, but we need to rise into the vision and just do it! Will you rise up into the vision God has for you?

SUPPLEMENTARY QUESTIONS TO CHALLENGE AND INSPIRE

How was Gideon's faith activated?

How will you activate your faith?

Dreams and visions bring us revelation from God. How do we test and confirm our divine leading?

What do you see as your inheritance in God? What changes will it mean in your life for you to do the works that Jesus did?

HOW TO ACCELERATE, MOVE INTO HIGHER SPEED, FOR THE ANOINTING TO CHANGE AND OPERATE IN OUR LIVES

"You only need five minutes for the power of God to fall," Bry said.

"That's what you need."

"Come on," I said. "That's okay for you, you are used to that, but for me, it's a different story!"

We stood in the dark with a lantern. I looked out on this almost completed building, filled with people. People were everywhere, even looking in the windows. A sense of excitement, expectancy arose within me. At 11:25 p.m. on New Year's Eve, I knew we must finish by midnight. I spoke for just five minutes and called for people to respond and come forward.

Kate sang a beautiful song. "Come, Holy Spirit, I need you. Come, sweet Spirit, I pray. Come in your strength and your power. Come in your own special way."

Everyone came, and so too did the power and presence of God. God moved, and many fell to the floor with His wonderful presence. Jesus transformed and changed lives.

Unbelievers came in off the street and crowded to the front because the glory of God was there. They reported that never had they felt such a great power. Many saw visions and bright lights. People said they evidenced a tremendous presence. Goose bumps appeared on their arms, and the hairs on their arms stood up on end! The Holy Spirit came in power. He moved amongst the people with many falling under the power of God and being set free from curses over their lives.

The message had been about surrender, and the entire congregation responded by coming to the front. I imagined it must have been like the early days of the Pentecostal revival, and it filled me with awe, that God would take women from New Zealand, moving by faith in obedience to his word, to this island on the other side of the world. God wants to use everyone as we become extraordinary when we come to know Jesus as Lord and Savior.

When I had visited this church the year before, it was a decrepit old ruin. For forty years, the government forbade churches in Cuba to undertake maintenance. Now a large two-storied concrete building was built by faith to seat one thousand people, built in response to a prophecy three years before. The pastor shared how the prophecy said one day he would build a large church in this city to which people from most walks of life would come. "Today this prophecy is being fulfiled in your eyes," he stated.

Unbelievers came in off the street and reported that the hairs on their arms stood on end. A young man, a nonbeliever, saw a brilliant ball of light over the church, and someone saw tongues of fire on our heads.

PALMAS

That night a tall upright woman came forward. The next morning the pastor shared the lady, an avowed communist, had come to him, saying, "You know, I do not believe, that I am a communist woman. Yet after I walked forward, I woke on the floor as though I floated on a cushion with the presence of a great power."

The pastor said, "Never has there been such a move of God like this in my church. I knew people fell down but thought it would never happen here and never to me. Please forgive my people, everybody wants to be at the front because of the wonderful presence of God."

At midnight, the rejoicing began as we welcomed in the New Year, thanking God for what he had done and what he had ahead for us all.

In this nation of Cuba, I learnt much about how to move in the anointing of God and listen to the Holy Spirit.

After the first trip, in August 1992, the Rhema broadcast had only just finished when the phone began ringing. An older lady of eighty-two years from Hastings phoned, wanting to go to Cuba. In the conversation's course, she suggested I should read the book by a well-known author about the Holy Spirit and immediately mailed it to me. I did not know of this man, but I read the book with much interest and bought the next one he wrote on the anointing. These books increased my hunger for God and revealed to me I had been part of a tremendous move of the Holy Spirit during my time in Cuba a few months before.

A car stopped in the drive outside the window. Our daughter and son-in-law had arrived. Reluctantly, we turned off the video we had been watching. After reading the books, we hired many of these videos that were to change our lives forever. As I sought the Lord and knelt on the floor while the videos played, the Holy Spirit came in the room and touched me. The tangible presence of God came. The more I watched, the more I sought the Lord, and the more God came. Never had I experienced such a phenomenon with videos! Rebecca and Arjay said later, when they entered the house, they could hardly stand up because of the power of God! When friends phoned me, they heard the video playing in the background, and they said, "Are you watching another video?" We couldn't get enough, we were hungry for God. Daily I cried out to God and sought to yield and surrender to him more.

Shortly after the Rhema broadcast, we were invited to Rotorua to speak at a small church. A great service and the ministry time came. There, it began deliverance, healings; the power of God startled me. People fell everywhere. It changed their lives.

With the precious holy anointing of God, we change gears and pick up speed. After the Holy Spirit fills us, we are to move in the anointing of God and accelerate in purpose.

God doesn't look at our ability but at our availability. When we say, "Lord, I'm available," he puts into us his ability to do his work. We call the impartation of his ability into our lives to do his work, the anointing. The word "Christian," in Greek, means the anointed one (Strong's).

I'm just a woman who said, "Just do it, Lord. I'm available. Use me. I'm nothing. I'm nobody. I've no ability. I give myself to you. Use me. I'll do whatever you want me to do."

God took me at my word when he imparted his ability into my life. In these last chapters, we will look at an acceleration in purpose. We recognise the importance of changing gear to enable us to move on with greater speed and safety to achieve our goal.

How did God do it? What did God do? Why did God do it? What happened as a result? But first, I want to share briefly a little of my walk with Jesus. Who am I?

Married for over fifty years, with two grown children with teenage families, the entire family follows Jesus. I became a Christian at nine and a half years, the first Christian in my family. Because of my conversion, my entire family came to faith. Just an ordinary woman working as a nurse educator, I regarded myself that way until 1989, when God spoke, calling me to the nations.

I decided I would go with a friend to the Anglican church just down the hill. I liked it and attended regularly. With no encouragement at home, as my father had been a Catholic, but finding no relationship with God believed nothing. My mother, brought up in a Christian home, had never found a relationship with Jesus. She had known about him but never turned to him for help, even when, at sixteen, her mother had died, leaving her, two younger sisters, and a brother orphans.

As the months passed, I came to a growing realisation that Jesus had died for me, and gradually, as the truth of the word of God soaked my life, I became a Christian. The well-known writer and Anglican statesman John Stott came to the church, and that night I made a public commitment of my life to Jesus Christ. I remember well the scripture the Lord gave me:

> "Being confident of this, that he who began a good work in you will carry it on to completion until the day of Christ Jesus" (Philippians 1:6 ESV).

At thirteen, God spoke and called me to serve him. I read three inspirational books about three Jewesses who found and served Jesus. These had touched my life, and I prayed and read missionary books, attended missionary meetings, and even joined a mission group praying for Israel and the Jews. My heart burnt with fire for the nations. I believed I would go as a missionary to serve the Lord in the nations. But years and much of my life passed before this call came to fruition.

As I have shared in previous books, *Heavenly Kaleidoscope* and *Endless Safari*, it resulted from a trip to Myanmar in 1989, that God spoke and called me to the nations and especially to Cuba. I could never have dreamt or imagined what God would do!

Let's look at the acceleration the anointing brings and what moving in the anointing means. It's about changing gear to move faster, with speed and precision, to reach the prescribed goal.

The anointing of God is precious and holy. It is such a precious thing that God puts on his servants, that he expects consecration.

Leviticus 8:30-35 (ESV) tells us that Aaron was told the anointing was so holy, he could not leave the temple/tabernacle for seven days, or he would die. They sprinkled the special anointing oil on Aaron's head, on his garments, and upon his sons and their garments. The holy anointing oil ran down his garments from his head to his feet and onto the floor. The oil did not touch his flesh. This reminds us that the Holy Spirit has nothing to do with the flesh! Moses took the oil, and the blood was on the altar. Where the oil is, the blood is; the Holy Spirit comes. Aaron and his sons were sanctified, set apart for God.

One year in Cuba, in obedience to the stirring of the Holy Spirit, I prayed for people and constantly spoke the blood! I had read a little book *The Blood* by Maxwell Whyte during my brief stay at West Palm Beach on the east coast of America as I prepared to enter Cuba. This book had blessed me and given me a tremendous revelation of the power there is when we speak the blood of Jesus over people and situations. I saw again and again the combination of the anointing and the blood. In Cuba, a woman slithered across the floor, writhing like a snake, in and out of the rooms in this decrepit rotting building. We followed her, speaking the blood of Jesus. Demons had manifested during the ministry time, and after speaking over her, using the power there is in speaking the blood, she experienced deliverance and freedom.

When we are anointed, it sets apart us to the Lord as a king or queen are, who, when appointed, are anointed to their authority and purpose. God appoints and then anoints us to set us apart for his service. With the anointing comes responsibility. We have a responsibility to spend more and more time with the Lord.

RESPECT THE ANOINTING

The anointing that God places on his people is so holy that he warned others against touching his anointed ones.

Miriam disobeyed God, and she learnt the hard way (Numbers 12:1-15 ESV). God judged Miriam and Aaron. They had no respect of the anointing upon Moses; they attacked him because of his marriage. Annoyed with Moses, they spoke against his actions. God would have killed them, but Moses intervened; he prayed. God struck Miriam with leprosy because of her sin, and she had to wait outside the gate until clean. Everyone knew of her sin. There must have been considerable shame for this rebellion, but Moses spoke on their behalf.

Leviticus 10:19 (ESV) tells us that Aaron's sons offered strange, unholy fire before the Lord. As a result, fire came forth from the Lord and killed them. They had no respect for the anointing; they tried to please God their way and not God's way.

Saul had no respect for the anointing. He offered unholy fire (1 Samuel 13 and 15 ESV). We must stay within and not move out of our anointing. We need to be hungry for God.

In Acts 5, Ananias and Sapphira lied to the Holy Spirit and did not respect the Holy Spirit or the anointing on Peter. As a result, they died! We must be obedient to what the Holy Spirit is saying. We must be honest. He wants us to be humble. We are to clothe ourselves with humility. God resists the proud. God looks at the heart (1 Peter 5:5-6 ESV).

In 1 Samuel 24:6 (ESV), David crept up unnoticed and cut off the corner of Saul's robe. Afterwards, conscience-stricken, he said to his men, "The Lord forbid that I should do such a thing to my master, the Lord's anointed, or lift up my hand against him, for he is the Lord's anointed."

In 1 Samuel 26:9, 11 (ESV), David said to Abishai, "Do not destroy him for who can raise his hand against the Lord's anointed, and be guiltless." Again, in verse 11, David says, "The Lord forbid that I should raise my hand against the Lord's anointed!"

Saul sought to kill David, chased after him, jealous of his anointing. He resented David, allowed anger against David to control him, and spoke against him. Despite this, David recognised the anointing of God upon Saul and would not usurp that position. It was there for the taking, as he could have killed Saul! One could almost have asked, "Has God delivered Saul into David's hands?" David refused to take the kingdom illegally or by violence.

It seems to me there is a dearth of teaching concerning these issues. Perhaps if there were more, there would be less hurt leaders in the body of Christ and more submitted believers!

> For whoever touches you, touches the apple of his eye.
> (—Zechariah 2:8 ESV)

> Touch not My anointed ones, and
> do My prophets no harm.
> (—1 Chronicles 16:22 ESV)

We must be very careful that we don't disrespect the anointing on someone else, or we will lose our own. God closely watches over his servants. We must be careful not to speak against anointed people, or judgement will be on us. Because Miriam became leprous, though a woman of God, they cast her out of the camp until she became clean! Let us be careful what we say about and do to people who carry the anointing.

Yes, this anointing is a tangible measure of God's Holy Spirit imparted upon those he has chosen. This anointing gives them the special supernatural ability to fulfil God's call upon their lives. Everything about the Holy Spirit comes to us. We cannot receive the anointing unless the Holy Spirit is within us, which happens at conversion.

WHO THEN HAS AN ANOINTING?

> See, I have called by name Bezalel the son of Uri, son of Hur, of the tribe of Judah, and I have filled him with the Spirit of God, with ability and intelligence, with knowledge and all craftsmanship. . . .
> (—Exodus 31:2-3)

> Choose seven good men of good and attested character and repute, full of the Holy Spirit and wisdom.
> (—Acts 6:3 ESV)

Stephen was amongst these men. The Apostles gave the anointing for service through the laying on of hands. Restoration of the laying on of hands came in the last century, as they lost the doctrine for hundreds of years.

It says in 2 Corinthians 1:21 (ESV) it is God who has consecrated and anointed us with the gifts of the Holy Spirit.

In 1992, after the first trip to Cuba, I prayed for some companions to travel with, and God spoke to many women. They were a mixed bag! The older lady mentioned previously, who God used marvelously, brought us into a fresh revelation of the Holy Spirit. Another woman said she would come, and her husband would come too. Only one problem: In a phone call to him, he said he was not a Christian, and neither of them were coming. Another woman phoned on the eve of our departure to say God had spoken to her, but she had done nothing about it!

Many are called, appointed, but few really move in the anointing! Many hear the voice of God, but few obey as few will pay the price.

We left New Zealand on 29 December that year, four women, for a month in Cuba, and for some of them, it became a baptism of fire! We were to experience the power of God splendidly.

THE ANOINTING OF THE HOLY SPIRIT ALWAYS PRODUCES POWER

The word "power" comes from the Greek *dunamis*, meaning ability, a force, special miraculous power (usually by implication a miracle itself), power, strength, violence (Strong's).

God's imparts his ability through the anointing. Anointing is defined as the enablement or impartation of God's ability upon an available and yielded vessel to fulfil and carry out his will and his work; to do supernatural work even though remaining natural beings.

Holman's dictionary's describes "anoint" as the procedure of rubbing or smearing a person or thing, usually with oil. This is for the purpose of healing, setting apart, or embalming. A person can anoint himself, be anointed, or anoint another person or thing.

While olive oil is the most common element mentioned in the Bible for anointing, oils produced from castor, bay, almond, myrtle, cypress, cedar, walnut, and fish were also used. In Esther 2:12, for example, they use the oil of myrrh as a cosmetic.

The Hebrew verb *mashach* (noun, *messiah*) and the Greek verb *chrio* (noun, *christos*) are translated "to anoint." From ancient times, they ceremonially anointed the priests and kings as a sign of official appointment to office and as a symbol of God's power upon them. It imbued the act with an element of awe. David would not harm King Saul because of the anointing the king had received (1 Samuel 24:6; Holman's).

In the New Testament, anoint is used to speak of daily grooming for hair (Matthew 6:17), for treating injury or illness (Luke 10:34), and for preparing a body for burial (Mark 16:1). Anointed by the Holy Spirit, we are being prepared for burial, the death of our flesh. Christians see Jesus as God's Anointed One, the Savior (Acts 10:38). God's presence and power are resident in the anointing. Likewise, the God anoints the Christian (2 Corinthians 1:21; 1 John 2:27 ESV) for the tasks of ministry.

Every born-again believer has an anointing.

> But you have an anointing from the Holy One, and you know all things.
> (—1 John 2:20 ESV)

It says in 1 John 2:27 (TPT) that the wonderful anointing you have received from God *is so much greater than their deception and* now lives in you. There's no need for anyone to keep teaching you. His anointing teaches you all that you need to know, for it will lead you into truth, not a counterfeit. So just as the anointing has taught you, remain in him.

This sacred unction abides permanently forever in you. Remain rooted in him, grounded, knit to him as he has taught you to do.

This is saying you and I have an anointing from the Holy One; he has given us an unction. This anointing abides in us for we have received the anointing from Jesus himself, and it is permanent. We have it forever. My anointing, given to me, is unique. Your anointing, given to you, is unique; it's your anointing.

People say, "I don't feel anointed." I want to tell you if I waited 'til I felt anointed, I would never pray for anyone. The anointing does not depend on our feelings. We decide and expect to be anointed. We put the anointing to work, as it's a decision to walk in the anointing.

There is no retreat, no debate. We tie the anointing to the word of God, standing on the word. As we live our lives by the anointing, we learn to walk by God's intention to walk in the anointing. The anointing abides in us, and out of our innermost being flows rivers of living waters. Nothing works without the anointing. We must base every decision we make on the anointing. The anointing to live is within us; the anointing to minister comes upon us.

Those whom God calls he also anoints. He doesn't ask us to do the impossible; he does that. The anointing calls everybody to change gear, to speed up, to accelerate to his purpose and plan!

Trip two to Cuba, I believed God for the team to go with me. That year $23,000 came in for the four ladies, including myself, to go. The youngest of the team, twenty-one years, only had her fare. On the day of departure, the church office phoned to say, "Come and collect a cheque!" Leaving the next day, I drove to get the cheque, $3,200! Praise the Lord, a woman changed it into cash for us to travel. Our God is the God of the impossible.

We were on the pavement in Havana, waiting for a van. Nearly an hour had passed as we waited in full view of everyone, four ladies, four enormous bags, and four backpacks! Too much luggage for a taxi! We passed through customs and passport control without having our bags opened. One tense moment came when they stopped us to enquire about one bag. They only wanted a baggage label turned around. These were bags full of precious Bibles, medicines, gifts for pastors in the nation.

TEAM IN MEXICO

KATE DENISE AND DEB OUTSIDE THE AIRPORT ON ARRIVAL IN CUBA

We waited and waited. On their first trip of this nature, the ladies were very anxious—arrived, but waiting for transport, yet not yet safe! Suddenly, a van arrived. And we breathed a sigh of relief as we hurriedly loaded our bags, pleased at last to get it out of the public view. I stood on the pavement, waiting, as the others clambered into the van. A tap on my shoulder made me freeze.

"Sister, I think I know you," a voice enquired.

To my relief, when I turned, a young man greeted me. We met the year before at his father's church on the city outskirts. This pastor had been of tremendous help to Fanny and me. On arrival, I aimed to contact him. I silently praised the Lord.

"Sister," he said, "come with me quickly. I have the car here. I will take you to my father."

After much persuasion, the reluctant ladies unloaded everything from the van. But great consternation at the size of the car! "No problem," Josh assured us. "You sit in the back and the bags go in the front seat and the boot." A feat, four of us in the back!

As we travelled along the bumpy roads, he told us the miracle of our arrival! They sent him to the airport at 9:00 a.m. that day to collect some people from Miami. He waited the entire morning and telephoned his father three times to say, "Can I come home? They are not coming, and I am hungry!"

His father kept telling him, "Just wait. They will come soon. Wait a little longer."

Yes, finally leaving the airport, they came, but not from Miami as expected! God had yet again proved his miraculous intervention and provision. With few cars on the road, shortly after our conversation, a car passed us going in the other direction. The driver waved out to us.

"That's my brother!" Josh exclaimed.

After thirty minutes' travel, we approached the church in an area of narrow streets full of large potholes. Finally, we stopped outside a compound with a narrow gate. Steep stairs led to an upstairs house. As we had turned the corner into the street, the pastor had appeared and ran down the stairs. We climbed wearily out of the car.

"It's you! It's you! It's you!" he shouted excitedly.

God sent four ladies from New Zealand!

So excited, Josh's brother phoned him, saying, "The people from Miami are on the way, the car is bulging, and there are bags and people everywhere!"

It amazed the pastor. He had just received a call from Miami to say the people had missed the plane and would not now be coming! It perplexed him. Who could be in the car?

"What a miracle," he said. "God sent Josh to the airport just for you!"

Even more of a miracle than we realised, the pastor whom I intended to visit by van had moved, and we would have had difficulties connecting with this man had we travelled by van! Praise God He does everything well.

When we move in the anointing of God, he anoints and appoints us for his purpose. He changes the gear from low and slow to overdrive, where we race along!

Excited, he shared that night at church, "It's a miracle!" He chuckled as he told the congregation. The people laughed and cheered at God's goodness and miracle-working power.

My eighth and final trip into China with Bibles, God had promised 100 per cent delivery this time. Flying back to New Zealand the following day, the organisation had asked me to do this trip and leave the other two ladies with a man coming off the next hovercraft. Returning with another man to Hong Kong on the same hovercraft, it sounded good!

We had travelled four hours to this entry point in this southern city in China. A first trip for the other ladies, one from Britain and the other from the United States. At passport control, we were separated because we were from different countries; no one would know we were travelling together.

I approached the X-ray machine, and to my consternation, the dreaded noise it sounded! *Beep! Beep! Beep! Beep!* I continued straight ahead as though nothing happened, but a woman from the counter waved me over. I obeyed and stood in front of her. She gestured to me to put the bag on the table. I did so, silently crying out to God, "Lord, you said 100 per cent this time!"

She looked at me, then gestured again for me to open the bag. I unzipped the zipper and stood there! She gestured to me to empty the bag. I did so. Slowly, I dragged the contents out one by one. I continued to pray and cry out to God, "Lord, the Christians here need this precious literature, and, Lord, you promised!"

There they were, two tin trays and two pot lids to block the X-ray waves, a lot of old clothes, and stacks of Bibles! She turned and called to the other officials. About six of them gathered around, examining the literature, talking loudly. Finally, they put the books on the table and returned to their work. She gestured to me to replace everything in the bag. This surprised me, as usually they called for a big blue bag and tossed everything in it and gave you a chit to collect the package on the way out of the country. I thought, *Well, maybe they are taking my bag too. That's a problem!* When everything was returned to the bag, she gestured to me to take the bag and go!

Go! I couldn't believe it! I scampered off as fast as I could, not stopping 'til I reached the park where we had planned to meet.

"A miracle! We had miracles!" we exclaimed as we exchanged stories at the park.

The lady from England had a similar experience to me! The other lady, a very large African American, had walked straight through the customs and immigration hall without being seen. She did not show her passport or put her baggage on the X-ray. Our God is truly the God of miracles, who delights to do the impossible: an enormous woman who could never have gotten through unseen! When we go in obedience to the call of God, he anoints us and protects us for the task he has for us.

Let's look briefly at the anointing upon Jesus. He is our pattern. His life was never stationary, never on park, always changed gear—moving forward! He brought the kingdom to earth; heaven touched earth in his life.

He carried out his ministry through the anointing of the Holy Spirit. For thirty years, he pleased God, living a righteous and holy life. Then in John 1:30, when he met with John the Baptist and was baptised, Jesus received the anointing of the Holy Spirit (John 1:29–34 ESV).

In John 1:32 (ESV), the Holy Spirit descended from heaven like a dove, alighted upon him. The heavens opened, and John saw it. A voice spoke from heaven. God said he, Jesus, his son, pleased him. He found delight in him (Luke 3:22 ESV). God anointed Jesus with the Holy Spirit to die! Until then an ordinary man, he received power when the heavens opened and the Holy Spirit came upon him. The anointing of God came upon Jesus to enable him to do the works. There were three years of power-filled ministry as the Holy Spirit led and guided him (Matthew 4:1). Immediately, the Holy Spirit from within drove him out into the wilderness; there was immediate action (Mark 1:12 Amplified). He led him. Have you acted since the Holy Spirit came on you? The

Holy Spirit brought change to Jesus, and his intention is the same for us. He came up out of the wilderness full and controlled by the Holy Spirit, led by the Holy Spirit, under the power of the Holy Spirit (Luke 4:1, 14 Amplified). In him dwelt the fullness of the Godhead bodily. God's purpose sped up in his life as he sped up in the anointing.

Jesus himself said in

Luke 4:18 (TPT)(18-19)"The Spirit of the Lord is upon me, and he has anointed me to be hope for the poor, freedom for the broken-hearted, and new eyes for the blind, and to preach to prisoners, 'You are set free!'

I have come to share *the message of Jubilee*, for the time of God's great acceptance has begun." To send forth delivered those who are oppressed– who are downtrodden, bruised, crushed and broken down by calamity."

Without doubt, we can conclude the works of Jesus resulted from the anointing. The anointing enabled him to do the works he did. If Jesus said that we are to do the works and greater works he did (John 14:12), then that must mean we have the same anointing that he had. Nothing else will do. We can't do the works unless we believe and act. The same power available to Jesus is available to you and me to do the works of Jesus and even greater works than he did. We are heirs of the Father, joint heirs with the Son. God's Son Jesus is heir to everything God has. God gave to Jesus total power, absolute authority, tremendous might! We receive these through the precious Holy Spirit, indwelling us. Whatever Jesus did, he did not do on his own authority, but on the authority of the Father. As an heir, we have the same authority that Jesus had, and the Father does the works. We can do these things because of the person of the Holy Spirit indwelling us. If we want the same power that Jesus had, it must prepare us for the same pain (John 17:21-23, 14:10-12 ESV).

Jesus is the one who baptises in the Holy Spirit, and we receive the Holy Spirit by faith.

Acts 10:38 (ESV) says God anointed Jesus of Nazareth with the Holy Spirit and power, and God will do the same for you and me.

The following are some personal examples of moving in the anointing when ministering in the nations.

She was inconsolable as she wept and wept. The pastor's wife took her to the prayer room and beckoned to us to follow. "She is the elder's daughter, and her little girl is in hospital very sick," we were told. "She has been there for six weeks. The pastor has been to pray for her, but we want you to go."

We asked, "Is it all right? Can we go to the hospital?"

They said, "No, the government does not allow foreigners at the hospital, but we will pray. It's a long way. Be ready to go at 7:30 a.m. tomorrow."

The next morning, after a long walk, we arrived at the hospital, very rundown, unpainted, and in a poor state. They allowed us to enter and visit the child. We anointed the little girl with oil and prayed the prayer of faith. We quietly prayed and proclaimed the name of Jesus over her and told her body to come into divine order. We did not know the problem, Just that she had been in the hospital for six weeks and had almost died. Other mothers in the ward wanted us to pray for their children, and what a privilege to do this. We left speedily when we finished, as foreigners could not be there, illegal to be there!

Two weeks later, the excited mother came to church. She shared that they diagnosed her little girl with a malignant lung tumor. After we prayed, they had taken her to the city, one hour away, for major surgery. Prior to the operation, they X-rayed her lungs.

"Why have you brought her here?" they asked. "There is nothing wrong with her!"

That child, now a woman, is alive and well today in Cuba.

THE MOTHER AND CHILD

When we move in the anointing of God, we can bring release to the captives, we can lay hands on the sick, and Jesus will heal them.

> Hebrews 13:8 (ESV) tells us that Jesus is the same yesterday, today, and forever and forever and forever.

We were in a house church in Havana. An older man said to me, "Share how God healed you from cancer."

I told the people what God had done in my life, then I asked him to tell his story as the senior pastor had told me the amazing miracle. He said, "A member of the party, I had cancer of the kidneys, yet my father asked the pastor to visit me. It was difficult for him to come as the entire family were communists and they gathered around me. The pastor wanted to pray with me privately, but I did not understand that until later. They were very frightened as my family were party members! After the pastor and some church members prayed for me and explained the Christian message, I had surgery. They opened me up and closed me up! A hopeless case! Too advanced to be removed, the cancer infiltrated everywhere! Afterwards, I came to Jesus, and each day I improved and experienced total healing from God. As a result, God healed my father, who had a psychiatric disorder and could not speak properly. He and my entire family became Christians."

After we shared, the spirit of the Lord moved on the people. A spirit of prophecy came, and the people were weeping and praying—a holy time with the wonderful presence of the Lord. I cried out to God that out of our innermost beings would flow rivers of living water, and God made it happen. Much deliverance followed, many words of knowledge and wisdom and scriptures for the people as we worshipped the Lord. Finally, we stood in a circle and proclaimed the blood and sang, there is power, power, wonder working power in the Blood of the Lamb, as we stamped on Satan and declared his position is under our feet!

How wonderful our God is, how wonderful Jesus is, how wonderful the Holy Spirit is. He is a Holy Spirit, and when he comes, his beautiful presence brings the presence of Jesus.

THE MEETING AND PETE

We visited Nilia in Vladimir. Having no children, it shamed her, as Christian society had large families. After a criminal septic abortion, at fifteen years, she almost died. Now infertile, she felt despised and dirty. Her family, alcoholics who tried to kill her at birth, rejected her.

The actions of a caring neighbour saved her life. She lived a life of total rejection. What a wonderful time we had with her, as after she shared her heart, we prayed to break the curses of rejection, infertility, suicide, alcohol, woundedness, death, and hell. We spoke healing to her body and told her fallopian tubes and ovaries and uterus to come into divine order. Gloriously set free before our eyes, we rejoiced with her.

The following visit two years later, we praised God that she had become pregnant shortly after we left. What a miracle! God had answered her and our prayers, but she did not realise and lost the baby through carrying heavy things up many flights of stairs.

EVERYONE NEEDS THE ANOINTING OF GOD

Satan's burden will be destroyed because we have grown so fat with the anointing of God. The anointing of God breaks the yoke of bondage, obliterates and totally smashes the yoke. He cannot repair it (Isaiah 10:27 ESV).

Luke 24:49 (TPT) And I will send the fulfilment of the Father's promise to you. So stay here in the city until the mighty power of heaven falls upon you and wraps around you." Until you are clothed with power.

> And while staying with them, he ordered them not to depart from Jerusalem, but to wait for the promise of the Father, which, he said, "You heard from me; for John baptised with water, but you will be baptised with the Holy Spirit not many days from now." So when they had come together, they asked him, "Lord, will you at this time restore the kingdom to Israel?"
> (—Acts 1:4-8 ESV)

He said to them, "It is not for you to know times or seasons that the Father has fixed by his own authority. But you will receive power when the Holy Spirit has come upon you, and you will be my witnesses in

Jerusalem and in all Judea and Samaria, and to the end of the earth." Another translation says, the remotest areas of the earth, we are to receive the promise of the Father—ability, efficiency, and might—when the Holy Spirit comes.

Acts 4:29–31 (ESV), "Now, Lord, consider their threats and enable your servants to speak your word with great boldness." "Stretch out your hand to heal and perform miraculous signs and wonders through the name of your holy servant Jesus." "After they prayed, the place where they were meeting was shaken. And they were all filled with the Holy Spirit and spoke the word of God boldly."

He will clothe us with power from on high. When the Holy Spirit came to Gideon, he clothed him with himself and took possession of him (Judges 6:34 ESV). There will be boldness. We will witness fearlessly. We will receive power, efficiency, ability, and might. To have a move of God, we must change and allow God to change us.

Without the anointing, there is no power. Jesus knew power left him when the woman touched Him. She felt healed (Mark 5:29-30 ESV). Jesus calls us to move in power, to break the yoke of Satan over people's lives. Virtue is to flow out of us. The life of Jesus is in us. It's an exchange. He took our sin and gave us his life. Our old life is dead, it's gone, it's finished!

In Bulgaria, the people wanted to touch us! They regarded us as holy women and wanted to venerate us. Paul and Apollos had the experience in which the people wanted to worship them as gods. We must be careful to give the glory to God and point the people to Jesus; it's his power. When people touch us, the presence of God should flow out through us. People can touch us and be healed. When we prayed recently at a friend's home, she shared that when we touched her, fire burnt her body. Yes, God's word, spoken through men and women under the anointing of God, carries the same creative force as if God had spoken it.

The anointing to teach brings the revelation of God. The anointing to preach burns deep within us, and when we preach, it comes forth with significant power and always brings hearers to a decision for change.

> We are to stir up the gift of God that is within is and fan it into flame.
> (—2 Timothy 1:6 ESV)

The preaching came to a close. The crowded church had listened attentively. A woman had been crying out during the preaching. In Spanish, she said, "That's me, that's me, that's me!" I had been speaking on the blessings and the curses and the effects on our lives. She came for prayer during the ministry time and experienced glorious freedom and healing from hurts. We broke religious curses over her life. Born into the family of God, she gave her life to Jesus. The church rejoiced. The wife of their music leader, who, in the past year, had returned to following Jesus, after twenty years of sin and degradation. A year later, she led worship services. Praise God for his faithfulness as she, not a new Christian, became a mature woman of God. She discipled and led others to Jesus.

The anointing of God breaks every yoke of bondage. The anointing of God brings us into a power-filled life. When God calls, he anoints. With the calling of God to ministry comes the anointing for the ministry. We have to grow in it and then learn to move in it. We must know when the anointing is upon us and when it is not.

The four of us were sitting in our third-floor apartment room, resting and talking about the trip. One lady said, "I have never fallen under the power of God. Would you show me what you do and would you pray for me?"

I replied, "Okay. Stand right here." We stood up, and she stood in front of us. I said, "In the name of Jesus," and put out one finger to touch her forehead, and as I did so, she fell to the floor! We lifted her up from the floor amazed, and I said, "Okay, I'll show you again." This time I said, "In . . .," and she fell to the floor! The anointing of God is a manifestation of the power of God.

God does not show his power without his presence. His presence filled us wherever we travelled in Cuba, and it's the same here. He is with us and will move through us, manifesting his presence wherever we go.

Acts 1:8 (ESV) tells us that when the Holy Spirit (the presence) comes upon you, you shall receive power.

GOD DOES WHAT HE WANTS IN HIS OWN WAY!

The woman fell on a stack of people. People were everywhere! At the end of the preaching, the pastors and leaders had removed every seat out of the tiny church as we needed room to minister. We prayed for every person. The Holy Spirit moved mightily, and many people were lying on the floor, one on top of the other! She lay there, on the top! A man moved angrily towards her and reached out to pull her off the stack! But the pastor's wife and I simultaneously pointed to him and shouted, "No! No! Don't touch her!"

And as we did, the Holy Spirit took him and threw him across the room! He landed flat on his back about twenty feet from where he had been standing!

Where the spirit of the Lord is, there is boldness, power, authority, and love. The children's meeting had started twenty minutes late because of the power cuts. Except for a powerful kerosene lantern, darkness filled the church. With the use of a gospel glove, I told stories and shared how to come to faith in Jesus. What a wonderful response with many children born again.

The next service followed straight after with a full church. Before every service in this church, the pastor and people prayed for three quarters to one hour. The pastor had marched round and round the building, speaking the name and blood of Jesus.

I spoke on surrender and called the people to do so. This was on my first trip to Cuba. Not a preacher, I had never held an altar call and not for four hundred people!

I looked out into the dark church as I asked the people to respond by raising one hand if they wanted to give their life to Jesus. They raised every hand! I could not believe it and said to the interpreter, "We will say it again. Perhaps we did not make it clear." Carefully, I explained what it means to follow Jesus, and this time I asked the people who wanted to give their lives to Jesus to stand.

Amazed, at this, I thought maybe the interpreter had not interpreted what I said correctly. A lovely young man, a Baptist, saw me before the service when we discussed what we would say. He had never interpreted before and seemed to have a very good command of English.

"Tell the people to sit down," I said. "We will go through it again!" I explained even more carefully, and the people listened patiently. Finally, now I felt sure of myself, I said, "If you want to know Jesus in the way I have been talking about, please come forward." A stampede. The whole church responded! Freda, my companion from Canada, and I were pinned back against the platform, and there were people everywhere! The Holy Spirit moved wonderfully, and for me, it began the moving in a power anointing in Cuba. Every time I have been in that church in the island's east, God has done amazing things.

SANTIAGO DE CUBA

To move in the glory of God is to move in love and mercy.

When Moses had been with God, he did not know his face shone, but the people could see it. When he said, “Let me see your glory,” he forgot himself. God-conscious, he lost every bit of self-consciousness. Moses spent the first forty years of his life learning human wisdom, the next forty years knowing his helplessness, and the final forty living in the power of God. It took 120 years! (Exodus 33:18, 22-23; 34:29-30 ESV). We have to lose sight of ourselves and see only Jesus. People need to see on our faces we have been with Jesus.

We need to say, “Lord, I’m nothing. I want your presence, Lord. Let there be nothing of me.”

We need to be hungry for his presence. There needs to be total surrender. The amount of the glory of God that we show forth is directly proportional to our consciousness of God. The degree of anointing evident is in proportion to the degree of glory evident. We must move in divine love.

To develop God’s glory in us, it is important to spend time in his presence, read and meditate on his word, and suffer for Christ meekly, the reproach of being a Christian.

God demands everything—money, time, talents. It's not a harsh demand. He won't force us. It's always up to us. He set the example in giving his Son Jesus; Jesus, who gave everything for us, for you and for me; Jesus, who took upon himself the form of a servant and made in the likeness of man. He humbled himself and became obedient even unto death. Jesus died painfully on the cross. This is the most painful way to die. Jesus gave everything for you and me. We are to die daily and follow Jesus; we are to suffer and die daily to the flesh! The flesh has to die!

Philippians 2:5-11

And consider the example that Jesus, the Anointed One, has set before us. Let his mindset become your motivation. The Example of Jesus Christ He existed in the form of God, yet he gave no thought to seizing equality with God as his supreme prize. Instead he emptied himself of his outward glory by reducing himself to the form of a lowly servant. He became human! He humbled himself and became vulnerable, choosing to be revealed as a man and was obedient. He was a perfect example, even in his death—a criminal's death by crucifixion! Because of that obedience, God exalted him and multiplied his greatness! He has now been given the greatest of all names! The authority of the name of Jesus causes every knee to bow in reverence! Everything and everyone will one day submit to this name—in the heavenly realm, in the earthly. The authority of the name of Jesus causes every knee to bow in reverence! Everything and everyone will one day submit to this name—in the heavenly realm, in the earthly realm, and in the demonic realm. And every tongue will proclaim in every language: "Jesus Christ is Lord Yahweh," bringing glory and honour to God, his Father!

[TPT]

Yes, he wants our total consecration, our surrender, our total surrender. The level of our surrender shows the level of the anointing upon us. There is always more we can give. It's a process, always giving, yielding more and more to him, that Jesus will be present more and more in our lives.

It's a choice. We make choices. We choose total surrender! It's dying to what we are, what we were, and what we will be. Jesus wants the "I" in you and me to die. There is no other way for the beauty of Jesus to come forth. There has to be more of him and less of us. When he is satisfied that we are ready to give our whole being, not just a part, but also yielding everything to him daily, that's total, every part of our lives to his will, to perform his call, then and only then will his ministerial anointing come on us.

We must prepare, or there will be no anointing. We pay the price. I had to pay the price. The first major price to die to the vision and to life itself. When I had cancer, I cried out to God, "Do whatever you want to in my life." To die once is no use! It is only the beginning. We have to die to things we never dreamt would ever happen!

The phone rang. "Your mother has just gone to be with Jesus," my brother-in-law's voice at the other end said. That afternoon I flew to Otago for the second time in two weeks. I had almost not returned from the holiday visit to my elderly parents the previous week, as they seemed so frail and one in hospital!

The funeral and the tidying up of the belongings followed. It alienated my whole extended family! It stunned me! Not only did I lose my mother, but also relationships between myself and my only sister and her family were severed! Two weeks later, the phone rang again. This time my stepfather had gone to be with Jesus. I decided not to go back to the traumatic situation! The pastor and a friend intervened. "You must go," they said. "You must see it through."

I leaned on the Lord and flew south. On arrival, the girls apologised and told me they loved me. Reluctantly, I stayed with the family for a few days until I could escape to my mother-in-law's house after the funeral.

Three weeks later, broken, I travelled to Cuba! I walked away from everything that belonged to my mother. I left the family in the hands of God and prayed that God would bring the healing and reconciliation necessary.

> God wants us to be broken vessels before he can pour out his anointing. The alabaster bottle had to be broken before the beautiful fragrance could be released

I sat in the church in Hamilton late one night with the two pastors. Tears poured down my cheeks. "I never asked for this anointing!" I cried. "I never asked to be called!"

"Neither did we," they both agreed.

"It's so painful," I cried.

People were gossiping and criticising me, and no matter what I did, people criticised. I said to them, "Please allow me to go to each of the ladies in leadership in the church. Let me ask them to speak into my life. Let me ask them to forgive me if I have done anything to upset or wound them."

Not permitted to go to the ladies' group, I met with the key ladies in that church and did just what I asked. I believed this action of humbling myself brought a measure of healing to the situation, but my friend came to me a few months later to say, "It's no better, there are still problems."

In 1997, this situation cost me the credential I had with the church to which I belonged. Again, I had to die, to my reputation, to my ministry, to my credibility, to the future.

It's painful to die! We have to die alone. You know it's not what happens to us that matters; it's what we allow it to do in us. Jesus is to be seen in us. That fragrance from the myrrh of suffering is to waft up from our lives and fill the place where we dwell. It is to rise as a sweet offering to Jesus.

The Father despised Jesus when he took our sin upon himself. We may have to be despised by others and suffer reproach as a Christian for our walk and beliefs in the Lord. Jesus learnt obedience by the things he suffered (Hebrews 5:8).

The Cuban church suffered much reproach, persecution, and suffering, especially over past years when the government has moved against it in fresh ways.

Jesus said in John 17:10 (ESV), "All I have is yours, and all you have is Mine." There is a perfect sharing. The measure of God's commitment to us is total. He gave his all for us. He gave his precious beloved Son. What level is our commitment to the Lord? All we have is his! Will we pay what Peter and Paul paid to have what they had?

To develop in the anointing, it's phase by phase, step by step, stage by stage, as it is changing gears. When we are obedient and faithful at each step, God leads us on to the next step. If we are disobedient, then we stop moving. We go into park—stationary and often accelerate in reverse. Disobedience stunts our growth. The level of the flow of the anointing is greater at each step, each phase. We have to pay the price to see God move.

Total surrender to see him move, that's what he asks. Are you willing to say, "Lord, I surrender?" He wants our entire lives.

In Genesis 32:24-32 (ESV), the heading in my Bible says, "Jacob is wrestling with God," but when you read it, really, it is God wrestling with Jacob until he has him. I know how this passage has blessed me as I have cried out like Jacob, "I will not let you go, Lord, unless you bless me." Jacob left alone, wrestled with a man until daybreak. The entire night the man wrestled with Jacob. Now when the man saw that he did not prevail against Jacob, he touched his thigh and caused Jacob's thigh to be out of joint.

The man said, "Let me go," but Jacob said, "I will not let you go unless you declare a blessing on me."

Jacob had a revelation of God, and he came out of this encounter limping, leaning on the Lord. God wants people who "limp" and, therefore, have to lean on him. Does God have you? Are you limping and leaning on the Lord?

I want you to ask yourself, "Am I anointed?" Some people would say it is presumptive to say so, that you are arrogant, full of pride, and boastful. People would say we don't have the right to say so. I don't agree with that.

A Christian is an "anointed one." Christ means the "anointed one." Jesus died for us, gave his entire life for us so we would become as 2 Corinthians 6:16 says, a temple of the Holy Spirit. We are the temple of the Living God.

> Your bodies are members, bodily parts of Christ the Messiah, one in spirit with Him, united to Him, He lives in you. (—1 Corinthians 6:15 ESV)

What do we think of when we hear this? Let us think for a few minutes about Peter. I remember Peter for his confession. "Thou art the Christ," he said to Jesus. What a statement! Think about Peter. Peter saw much. There, for that first miracle in Mark 2:11 (ESV), when the Jesus healed the paralytic; there, when they caught the fish and the nets were breaking in John 21:11 (ESV); again for the raising of the dead, when Jairus's daughter came back to life in (Mark 5 ESV). He saw the demons flee (Mark 9:17-29 ESV) and the money taken from the fish's mouth (Matthew 17:24 ESV) and there at the transfiguration (Mark 9 ESV). Peter knew what Jesus could do.

He knew what the anointing could do as he saw the power and the glory. It's easy to remember his denial, his faithlessness, his unworthiness, but when Jesus said Acts 1:5-8 (ESV) to him, imagine how he felt! John baptised with water, but you shall be baptised with the Holy Spirit not many days from now. And so when they had come together, they were asking him, saying, "Lord, is it at this time you are restoring the kingdom to Israel?"

He said to them, "It is not for you to know times or epochs which the Father has fixed by his own authority; but you shall receive power when the Holy Spirit has come upon you; and you shall be my witnesses both in Jerusalem, and in all Judea and Samaria, and even to the remotest part of the earth.

How would you feel? Excited, amazed, bold, fearless, ready, expectant, or scared, timid, frightened, hesitant, incredulous? It makes you think, doesn't it, and we should ask ourselves, why aren't we excited today?

Nothing could stop him. Acts 3 tells the story. He said boldly, "What we have we give you!" He knew what he had, and he gave it away! He had burden-removing, yoke-destroying, world-defying, devil-chasing, explosive, supernatural power. Such power flowing through his flesh, enabling him to do what the flesh cannot do.

In 1 Corinthians 12:7 (ESV), it speaks of the fivefold ministries. God gives the manifestation of the spirit to every man to profit withal… verses 8-10… we do not know exactly how the anointing will manifest, but by faith we believe and expect it will manifest. I never know what God will do. There is sometimes a surge of power when we change gear. We experience a surge of power when we move in the anointing.

The anointing abiding in you continually is received by faith (1 John 2:27 ESV). We move by faith and let it flow by faith. We move in it by faith. We stop hindering it by questioning, "Have I got it?"

We have to learn the secret of union with Jesus. Your character holds the anointing of God. Every believer can move in the anointing of God, if we choose we can have as much as we want. We have to change gear, recognising everyone. Every believer has the same power, the same Holy Spirit, and can do the works Jesus did. None is special. Jesus operated in the anointing through union with the Father (John 17:21–23 ESV). Jesus is in us. Gears give us potential to move. The anointing, fire, and glory are all gears that when we recognise the potential, if used, we can move on into significant power!

> If you love Me, obey Me, abide in My words" (John 14:15 ESV).

Early in all this, before we developed the ministry, I learnt a new relationship with Jesus when God showed me some things, a fresh way of praying and reading the Bible. I learnt to proclaim it aloud instead of reading silently, walking by faith (Hebrews 11:1 ESV). To grow in the anointing of God, we must have faith. God responds to believing faith. I agreed with God and changed my confession (Amos 3:3 ESV), putting on the whole armor of God daily (Ephesians 6:12 ESV).

Let's look now at some aspects of the believer's anointing or the anointing within.

THE BELIEVER'S ANOINTING

This is a primary anointing, which judges every other manifestation. This is the most important anointing of all; it builds others around this. This believer's anointing was not in evidence in the Old Testament. The Old Testament saints had an anointing upon them. This is an anointing within, and we can increase the anointing within. How can we increase the anointing?

Hebrews 5:14 (ESV) tells us that by eating solid spiritual food and no longer drinking the milk of the word like an infant, we train our senses and mental faculties by practise to discriminate and distinguish what is morally good and noble and what is evil and contrary either to divine or human law.

> In the Gospel a righteousness from God is revealed, a righteousness is by faith from first to last just as it is written, the righteous shall live by faith.
> (—Romans 1:17 ESV)

Three times this verse is written in the Bible. This shows the principle of faith must be very important and the fact that we are righteous (Habakkuk 2:4, Hebrews 10:38 ESV). Another translation says, "My righteous one will live by his faith." Abraham was known as righteous Abraham because of his faith. We cannot please God without faith; it makes us righteous. The Amplified says, "This righteousness springs from faith and leads to faith. It is disclosed through the way of faith that arouses to more faith. The man who through faith is just and upright shall live and shall live by faith."

> Out of His fullness we receive and are supplied with, one grace after another and spiritual blessing upon spiritual blessing and even favor upon favor and gift heaped upon gift.
> (—John 1:16 ESV)

> As we behold in the Word of God the glory of the Lord, as in a mirror we are constantly being transfigured into His very own image, in ever increasing splendour and from one degree of glory to another. We are being changed to be like Him.
> (—2 Corinthians 3:18 ESV)

In our journey, when we are changing gear, we grow in faith in several ways.

Growth in Faith. We can all grow in faith. Faith is a manifestation of the Holy Spirit. There is no power without faith (Romans 12:6 ESV). The anointing we operate in is proportional to our faith level. The level of the anointing depends on the level of faith. A man, a woman, full of faith is also full of power and the anointing.

Since 1992, when I first visited Cuba, we have seen God do amazing things. Cripples walked, miracles signs and wonders happened. In this island nation, where Christians have been severely restricted since the communist revolution in 1959, God is moving. Believers have been imprisoned, persecuted, and churches destroyed for over sixty years. Despite communism and persecution, 59 per cent of this nation is Christian. Cuba is a land where the churches are full to overflowing, thousands are turning to Christ, crowds of people meet to pray for an hour or more before services. One church we visited has had two thousand new members in a year, the church only held four hundred, but there were sixteen cell churches, and people healed when they walked by on the street. The cell church movement gained momentum, with two churches in one year having twenty and twenty-six cell churches. Children with their own cells move in the gifts of the Holy Spirit.

Amongst the most wonderful times in Cuba were the beautiful moves of God on the children. Children, hungry to surrender, came forward at service after service, and the Holy Spirit moved upon them most beautifully.

When we move in the anointing, God uses us in most amazing ways. During the trips to Cuba, entire congregations everywhere congregations responded. Hundreds were healed, delivered, and set free; scores became believers, and hundreds fell under the power of God.

No water! And four ladies from New Zealand were about to arrive. The pastor and his wife prayed, "Lord, we need water, please send some rain." They knew how difficult it would be for these ladies with no water for their three-day stay. Shortly before our arrival at the church, the heavens opened with a torrential downpour of rain, enough to fill up their tank and supply all our needs for the complete stay.

On the way to this new area, we had to cross the steep mountains. The road, although in reasonable condition, was very dangerous. Unfortunately, the old and poorly maintained trucks and cars are hazardous on the road, causing terrible accidents.

The Volkswagen Golf car halted on a steep incline. We piled out, six of us! After a brief examination, the pastor solemnly told us, "The clutch cable has broken!"

We prayed for him to find a piece of wire to tie to the broken cable. He could find none and searched the car twice, as we kept on praying. Then he found a piece of wire he tied it on, and we jumped in! Horrible, the car would not start! We pushed it and jumped in. Still no good. This time it wouldn't go into gear. He said, "We must push it to the top of the hill! We groaned. How will we do it? The hill vertical and the top still about 300 m away! We prayed and spoke the word of faith. "Lord, we will get this car to the top of the hill!" When we pushed it, it appeared God took control of the car, and he pushed it up the hill as though on angels' wings!

At the top, we hurriedly piled in. "There is no clutch," said the pastor as we hurtled down the steep incline. "And there are no brakes!"

We cried out to God to protect us and prayed in tongues each time he changed gear! We spoke by faith. "Lord, we will get to Baracoa today! We will walk on the streets of Baracoa today."

Forty-five minutes later, after a five-hour journey, exhausted with the battle, we entered the city safely. Alleluia! He told us later the tyres were bare, and he prayed as we came, "Lord, don't let it rain!"

It is never possible to buy goods here, but that afternoon, he visited shops and purchased a new clutch cable for his old car! What a day of miracles! Faith is an attribute of the presence of God. If we spend more time hearing God's word, we will have more faith; we can increase faith.

> Faith comes by hearing and the message is heard through the word of Christ. (—Romans 10:17 ESV)

Romans 12:3 (ESV) speaks of the measure of faith. We all have the same measure which we receive at conversion, and we grow in it. As faith increases, the anointing increases, but faith means nothing if you don't know the grace of God. Romans 12:6 speaks of grace and faith being tied together.

Growth in Grace. We are to grow from grace to grace. The operation of the anointing is related to the operation of grace (Romans 12:6 ESV).

Ephesians 2:8 (ESV) tells us we are saved through grace, the undeserved favor of God. Paul became a servant of the gospel by the gift of God's grace.

Ephesians 4:7 (ESV) says unto everyone of us is given grace according to the measure of the gift of Christ.

The word *grace* means enablement, ability, or anointing (Brown). Grace can be multiplied and increased through the knowledge of Jesus (2 Peter 1:2-4 ESV). We need to be hungry for more knowledge of Jesus. We need to hunger and thirst after righteousness that we may be filled. We can grow in grace, and when we do, we grow in the anointing (2 Peter 3:18 ESV).

Growth in Glory. This produces an increase in the anointing, the glory of God and the anointing are directly related. When the anointing of God fills a place, it manifests the glory of God. This is the presence of God.

The spirit of glory and of God rests upon us (1 Peter 4:14 ESV).

It is the glory of God that causes people to fall under the power of the Holy Spirit. An increase in glory in our lives will produce an increase in the anointing. We can increase this anointing (Acts 2:2, 4:31, 16:26; Romans 6:4, 8:11 ESV).

What then can the anointing do? When preaching the gospel, cast out demons, speak in new tongues, take authority over serpents, give immunity to poison, and bring recovery to the sick through the laying on of hands (Mark 16:15-18 ESV).

The anointing within will produces a Christlike character, produces the fruits of the spirit. God will not trust us with his power unless we have the fruits of the Holy Spirit: love, joy, peace, faithfulness, meekness, self-control, kindness, and goodness. We want to develop the character of the Holy Spirit through leading a life in which we agree with the word of God, developed by meditation on the word, and by consistent committed prayer. All impressions received should be checked by the inner witness.

To move in the glory of God is to move in love and mercy. The glory of God brings the presence of God. We walked into a church in a small town in the Cuban countryside. The pastor's wife, an older woman, came towards me, and when we greeted, we hugged and hugged and hugged. The tangible love of God flowed. There was such a presence of his love. The next day she shared how for months before we came she had suffered with severe pain and high fevers. She knew it was the devil but could do nothing about it. She felt so helpless and was crying out to God, "Lord, I want to die, I can't take any more. Lord, please take me home!" She said she felt as though her heart was breaking, and from the moment we hugged, the symptoms left her, and she never again had the problems. She was totally healed. God's love and compassion reached out and touched her. Praise the name of Jesus who acts on behalf of those who wait on him. His power and presence will flow through us. We just have to be yielded and available (1 Corinthians 13). We must move in the love of God.

The increase in the anointing's level depends on us, on you and me. The responsibility to increase it is ours. We can increase it to the level Jesus had. We can do the works that Jesus did. When we experience the anointing, it is tangible; we can know it. As it is a supernatural feeling, I feel the anointing. Everyone experiences the anointing differently. We cannot put God in a box as he does things differently every time. Sometimes when I pray for people, I speak the blood, other times the name of Jesus, sometimes I blow or hit them, other times I touch only with one finger. We are to be sensitive to the leading of the Holy Spirit as to what we do and do what he says.

The day the cripple walked, we were sitting having lunch with the pastor's family at the back of the church when the anointing came upon me unexpectedly, and one arm and leg shook and vibrated. I said to those with me, "God is going to do something great today, look at me!"

It can manifest as extreme heat, where we get hotter and hotter. We can shake. My husband Kevin gets an intercessory anointing when I am speaking, and at meetings, he bends over at the waist and quakes! I asked him one day, "Does it hurt?" as it didn't look comfortable.

He said, "If it goes on the entire day, my body gets exhausted."

Elisha felt the anointing, and he knew when the anointing was not there (2 Kings 3:14, 15 ESV). He knew how to bring down the anointing. A musician played.

In Cuba, Kate sang "Come, Holy Spirit," and the Holy Spirit came; we wooed the Holy Spirit. In Cuba, people fell under the power of God with no one there to catch them as they bounced on concrete. It must have been just like where the priests could not enter the temple because of the glory as recorded in 2 Chronicles 5:14 (ESV).

Falling under the power is a side effect of the manifestation of the glory of God (Exodus 40:34-35 ESV). Some people receive a special blessing.

Remember the communist woman mentioned earlier? A young woman came one morning as I sat upstairs in the church, reading my Bible. She said, when she fell on the floor under the power of God, it seemed like chains fell from her arms. Afterwards, she felt light, bright, and free!

Not everyone who falls is changed or transformed. A friend of mine told me she had fallen down many times but had felt nothing special and did perceive herself not different for the falling!

Many years ago, when apart from Kevin for that eighteen months, I attended a convention, and during that time, I spent every day and evening of the ministry time on the floor. As though on God's operating table, it changed me! God did a work of healing in my life that I believe could not have happened any other way. As it soaked me in the anointing, God worked in my life.

We cannot establish a person's spirituality by whether they fall. Kevin had an experience where several pastors gathered around, praying for him. When he did not fall down, they said, "He is resistant," and prayed against resistance! The pastor ministering that night came and blew on him, and Kevin said, "An icy wind hit me full blast, and I could no longer stand."

In the Bible, there are many examples of people falling down. Daniel fell, Ezekiel fell, evil men fell (Ezekiel 1:28B, Daniel 10:7-9, John 18:5-7 ESV). When the Lord appeared to Saul, he fell down (Acts 22:6-9, 26:12-19 ESV). It's not an experience to be sought, just as an experience. In Cuba, everyone wanted it. A young man who kept coming forward seemed very disappointed when he did not fall down. The manifestation of the anointing is to destroy the works of the devil; we are to see people set free. We wrestle against principalities and powers (Ephesians 6:10-12 ESV). If people only fall on the floor and do not experience God, I believe we are wasting our time! My prayer is that it may change every person from glory to glory! Remember, every time God reveals himself, there is a purpose.

We have a responsibility to grow and develop within the set callings of God. God sets our limits when he places his call upon our lives. We need to recognise what office he calls us to function in. By office, I mean that spoken of in Ephesians 5, the apostle, prophet, evangelist, pastor, teacher. God gives these gifts.

We should understand what it means to be one of these. These are special offices, gifts to the body of Christ. Smith Wigglesworth, an apostle of faith, moved in tremendous power. Only some people are apostles, prophets, pastors, teachers, evangelists, but every one of us with the gifts of the Holy Spirit can do the works.

Every believer receives the life of Jesus when we are born again. We receive the gifts of the Holy Spirit and fruit of the Holy Spirit when we are filled with the Holy Spirit and we grow in them. All believers are anointed, appointed to do the works that Jesus did. There are no special people.

The senior pastor shared how God spoke prophetically that there would be a large church to seat one thousand people who would come from all walks of life. Someone had given him a car, so he felt to sell this to get the building started. Later a man from America gave him money for a car. Again, he seeded the money into the building. Today a beautiful church meets in a beautiful building in the city of Palmas, Cuba, because people faithfully gave and because of this faithful man.

Knowing God's Timing. The call and the anointing may come many years apart. Paul was forty-two years old when he was anointed at Antioch, yet God called him in his mother's womb and then again as a young man (Galatians 1:15, 16; Acts 7:58 ESV). Elisha prepared for years alongside Elijah. We should spend time alongside anointed people. The anointing is for service. We find our anointing in our calling. Find your calling. Do you know what your calling is? Are you an apostle, evangelist, prophet, teacher, or pastor? Ask God to show you, and when you find it, move in it.

Disobedience caused issues. Saul lost the anointing as did Uzziah (1 Samuel 13:9; 2 Chronicles 26:18 ESV). We spoke of this earlier, the price of failure to obey.

The keys to moving in and on with a ministerial anointing are faithfulness, patience, and waiting on God in worship. With each phase of obedience, God manifests a gift of greater anointing.

HERE ARE SOME KEY AREAS THAT WILL AFFECT THE LEVEL OF ANOINTING FLOWING IN ANY MEETING

Hunger level. The Cuban church is hungry for God. There are few Bibles. Many believers in the restricted nations do not get their own Bible until they are baptised or even for years after, as there are just not enough Bibles. A new convert has eight months of classes after conversion before they get a Bible! Prayer services are every day and meetings most nights. Crowded churches have people looking in the windows. In a crowded church with people hanging in the windows when we worshipped and prayed, twenty-five people came to faith in Jesus. People want more of God. Every child lines up for ministry, and it is wonderful to see God move upon the children. Some house churches throughout that nation have been closed by the government as the growth has been explosive (Acts 10:1, 2 ESV).

Prayer level of the early church (Acts 4:31-33 ESV). In Cuba, some churches always have people praying and fasting for the church through prayer and fasting chains. Before services, the people, not one or two, but most of the church, gather to pray.

Love and unity level. They were all of one accord (Acts 1:14, 2:1, 46 ESV). We experienced a wonderful service on the mountaintop. The spirit of the Lord moved among the people. As we clambered back down the mountain, we listened to the worship and praise, a majestic noise as people continued to surrender to the Holy Spirit. We had another meeting to go to, but the Holy Spirit continued to move in that place long after we'd gone because of the love and unity of the people.

Word and faith level. It builds the faith level up as signs and wonders happen. The woman with the issue of blood had faith. She reached out and touched the Lord. It took faith to do what she did. It wasn't just the reaching out to touch him; she went among the people, crawling through the crowd. Her determination brought her, her miracle! As an outcast, deemed unclean, the law forbade her to mix with people! But she dared to believe and acted on her belief (Mark 5 ESV). If you have watched Benny Hinn on video or television or been fortunate enough to go to a meeting, think about what you have seen. As the faith level builds, he encourages people to reach out for their miracle.

Worship level. As we worship the Lord, the level of the anointing in the meeting and in our time with God builds, increases. Private worship is a key to increasing the anointing in our lives. We need to reach out and worship more, in spirit and in truth, to come into the secret place with the Lord!

There can be fluctuations in the anointing. We need to recognise these. There can be "hot and cold" places in the anointing in buildings and meetings. We must wait on God to maintain the anointing.

Difficult, as it seemed like nothing happened, I had preached the word. A good number attended this prayer service. As I stood in the centre aisle of the church, I pondered what could be different. I felt to go up onto an elevated section at the side of the building, where the overflow crowd often sat and along which people visiting the pastor's rooms walked. I ministered, and the presence of God came most powerfully.

Sometimes, when we're ministering, there is the perception there is something more, that we are not finished. This happened to me in Guantanamo, near the U.S. Base. I almost completed the ministry time.

People had come to Jesus, others had been baptised in the Holy Spirit, delivered, healed, and set free, but it seemed unfinished. I handed over to the pastor, who then wept and cried out to God. A fresh move of the Holy Spirit began as the people too fell on their faces, weeping and crying out to God.

SOME PRINCIPLES TO INCREASE THE ANOINTING

Asking: The two disciples asked Jesus to stay, they constrained him, not knowing or recognising him (Luke 24:28-29 ESV). We need to learn how to keep the Holy Spirit's presence in the meeting; the presence of Jesus needs to be there when they come to us for personal ministry. We must search for him. God likes to hide himself (Isaiah 45:15 ESV). The longer we look for him, the more of the flesh dies. God is a gentleman; we must ask for what we need (James 4:2, John 16:23, 24 ESV).

Obedience: Let's be careful to listen to what the Lord is saying and do what he says! God gives the Holy Spirit to those who obey him. Obedience is better than sacrifice (1 Samuel 15:22; Acts 5:32 ESV).

Humility: There is no increase in the anointing without humility. When there is great anointing and power, it is because there is great grace. The only way to receive more grace is by the knowledge of him and by humility. Spiritual promotion by God comes only through humility (John 1:14; 2 Peter 1:2; 1 Peter 5:5 ESV).

Transference, Association: Elisha associated with Elijah. Timothy associated with Paul. The disciples associated with Jesus. The beautiful presence of Jesus, every one of his attributes, transferred itself (Acts 4:13 ESV). David became captain over five hundred social outcasts, yet they became mighty men of valour (1 Samuel 22:2; 2 Samuel 23 ESV).

There is a corporate anointing, where the leader brings the anointing and others in a team to move in that anointing. We can transfer the anointing to others who will then move in that anointing. This happened in Russia. We had only just five minutes to minister. I ran through the building, praying for the people. People fell in every direction! Total chaotic—noise, laughter, deliverance! I looked behind me. What happened to my companion? Afterwards, I asked her, "What happened to you? Why did you stop praying for the people?"

She said, "I didn't have the anointing!"

I said, "No, that's not true. Everyone has the anointing."

Later I thought about her statement, concerned, as I knew it to be incorrect that I be the only person ministering. God showed me what to do. The following night I called every leader and transferred the anointing to them, including the woman who travelled with me. We experienced no further problem.

If you want to move in the anointing, spend time with someone who does. In 2 Kings 1, the power of God Elijah had passed to Elisha. Elisha spent time with Elijah, and the mantle passed to him. The anointing, which means to rub or smear on, rubs and smears onto us from the person we spend time with. Read the books of the early revivalists and ask God for the same anointing. Watch the videos and cry out to God for the anointing.

Worship attracts God and the anointing of God. Worship creates a throne for God to sit upon on this earth. God inhabits our praises, and when God comes, the anointing comes. We wait on God by worshipping him (John 4:23, Psalms 22:3 ESV).

Retrospection: It's important to remember what happened and when, how the anointing came, what it felt like, and the way it operated. Paul reminded Timothy there are some things we are to remember. We are to be familiar with the experience of the anointing (2 Timothy 1:6 ESV). These examples in this chapter are examples of remembering and retrospection. On ministry trips, I always encourage my travelling companions to keep a diary for this purpose. I write many experiences and stories shared out of the diaries I have kept.

Word of God and Prayer: It takes faith to move in the anointing of God (Romans 10:17 ESV).

The word of God tunes our faith to move in the anointing (Romans 10:6). As we meditate on the word of God and digest it into our lives, more of the life of God is transmitted into us.

We function in the gifts in accordance with our faith.

"I prayed for the other secretary," Elena said. "I remembered what you said and did while travelling, I did it, and her headache left!"

We had just returned from ministry throughout Bulgaria with Elena, who interpreted for us. Her faith to believe had increased. Praise the Lord!

To maintain this anointing, we must fast and pray. I believe I need to do this regularly. We fast to see God move, to seek the face of God, to spend time with the Lord. I want to surrender to him in every area of my life. That is my prayer. Do you want this relationship?

He doesn't want the things we do for him; he wants our whole lives, our surrender (Philippians 2:5-11 ESV).

DAVID: A MAN WHO LEARNT TO SURRENDER

The anointing of God on David was powerful. The keys to this anointing were humility, sacrifice, and obedience. There were three stages. Samuel anointed him.

In 1 Samuel 16:1-19 (ESV), it tell us of the first anointing. This was God's sovereign choice, as he chose David, the least likely. The anointing is not dependent on ability, on who we are. His own father did not consider him, but God looks on the heart. He told Samuel, "I have chosen a man after my own heart."

For David, he had a time of preparation, a time of servanthood. After being anointed by Samuel, there were times of humility, obedience, and sacrifice. Life didn't change much, but he became different. This is an anointing of promise (1 Samuel 13:14 ESV). Then the wilderness experience, the struggle against the flesh where everything seemed to get worse Not yet a King, ruling and reigning over what! The desert, the caves, the difficulties, four hundred rebels!(1 Samuel 24:6, 1 Samucl 21:1-2; 2 Samuel 23:13 ESV).

David's second anointing was when all the elders Samuel anointed him king over Judah. They anointed him king, but for seven years, David ruled over just one tribe. We are to rule where we are. Judah means "praise." David was a man who brought praise and worship to the Lord. For a time of refining in the fire, he comes to Hebron, which means "the place of fellowship, the place of friendship." These are essential to kingship. We must come to the place of fellowship, friendship, intimacy with God. David knew what it meant to surrender (2 Samuel 2:11, 5:3 ESV).

In Psalm 42:7 (ESV), David says, "Deep calls unto deep, spirit calls unto spirit." He desired the presence of the Lord with all his heart.

Psalm 78:70-72 (ESV) speaks of David's walk with the Lord as a man of integrity. The greatest testing comes between the second and third anointing.

The third anointing, when they anointed David as king to rule over Israel, they anointed him this time to rule and to reign. He had to keep coming back to Hebron to keep close to God. God destines us to reign;

to be the head, not the tail; to experience glory; to be overcomers (2 Samuel 5:1-5; Hebrews 12:1-2 ESV).

The marks of the anointing in David's life were the spirit of the Lord came upon him in power, he played anointed music, he had great boldness with success in what he did. As a man of faith and vision, he knew his authority in God. He heard from God and sought him. While he knew the protection of God, he respected the anointing and strengthened himself in the Lord. With a humble heart, he repented to the Lord for sins committed. He worshipped the Lord, always faithful to his word. The keys to his life were obedience, humility, and sacrifice (1 Samuel 24:18-24; 1 Samuel 16:13-23; 1 Samuel 17:34, 35, 45, 46; 1 Samuel 18:14; 1 Samuel 24:6, 10, 26:9-10; 1 Samuel 30:6; 2 Samuel 6:12-23; 2 Samuel 9; 2 Samuel 12:13; Psalm 51; 1 Chronicles 14:10 ESV.)

Do you want the anointing?

> Be filled with Spirit.
> (—Ephesians 5:18 ESV)

Wigglesworth said, "Oh if you won't resist the Holy Ghost, the power of God will melt you down. The Holy Ghost will so take charge of you that he will fill you to the uttermost of His grace."

SOME QUESTIONS FOR YOU

The anointing is precious and holy. What do these scriptures say about this? Please see Leviticus 8:33-35, 10:1-9; Numbers 12:1-10; and 1 Chronicles 16:22.

Who has an anointing? Please see Exodus 31:2, 3; Acts 6:3; and 2 Corinthians 1:21.

Why do we need the anointing? Please see Luke 24:29, Acts 1:4-8, and Acts 4:29-31.

What is the secret to operating in the anointing? Please see Ephesians 6:12; Hebrews 11:1; and 1 John 2:27.

How is the anointing increased? Please see Hebrews 5:14; Romans 1:7; John 1:16; and 2 Corinthians 3:18.

Do we feel it differently? Do we have to grow in it? Here are some people who experienced the anointing: 1 Kings 19-2 Kings 1; 2 Kings 2:13–14; Isaiah 10:27; Jeremiah 5:14, 20:9; 1 Samuel 3:21, 10:10; 2 Samuel 23:2; Psalm 45:1; Daniel 10:10, 11; Ezekiel 3:14; Mark 5:29-30; Luke 24:32; Acts 1:8, 18:5; 1 Corinthians 2:4; 1 John 3:8.

Is the degree of anointing manifested proportional to the degree of glory manifesting? Please see Exodus 33:18, 22, 23, 34:6, 34:29-30:2; Chronicles 5:14, 7:1–3; Mark 16:17; and Romans 6:4, 8:11.

What is it necessary to have when we move in the anointing? Please see Acts 2:2, 4:31, 16:26; 1 Corinthians 13; 2 Corinthians 3:18; 1 Peter 4:14; and 2 Peter 1:4.

What do the scriptures say about falling under the power of God? Please see Genesis 2:21-22; Exodus 40:34-35; 2 Chronicles 5:14; Ezra 1:28b, 2:1; Daniel 10:7-9; John 18:6-7; and Acts 9:1-3, 4; 22:6-7, 9; 26:12-19.

Some keys affect the flow of the anointing. Please see Exodus 33:18; Isaiah 45:15; Luke 24:28-29; John 16:23-24; Acts 1:14; 2:1, 46; 4:31-33; 10:1, 2; James 4:2; 1 Peter 5:6; 1 Samuel 15:22; 2 Kings 3:11; Acts 5; John 1:14; 1 Peter 5:5; 2 Peter 1:2; 1 Samuel 22:2; 2 Samuel 23; Acts 4:13; Psalm 22:3; John 4:23; 2 Timothy 1:6; Romans 10:6, 17; and Philippians 2:5-11.

THE FIRE

When the fire comes, it touches and changes our lives. We are never the same again. God comes.

At midnight, we received a knock on the door, and when we opened it, breathless from our climb up the steep stairs a few minutes earlier, there stood the man from the front desk. Silently, he handed me a piece of paper. I returned to the room, shut the door, and opened the paper.

"I summon you to appear at the police immigration office at 10:00 a.m., Sunday. Signed, Alexo," the official message said.

We had just returned after a wonderful day in the city. This day had started at 7:00 a.m. at the praying service. There, many were ministered to, and the Holy Spirit had moved marvelously, bringing visions and tremendous release to those present. In the afternoon, we had travelled by jeep to an area outside the city, but the mud stopped us! We walked for forty minutes, crossed a bay in a rowing boat, and walked again to a little church in the countryside. After preaching and ministering, the glory of God came, and many found new life in Jesus.

MUD

We gazed at the summons in dismay, thoughts tumbling through our minds. It had been difficult since arrival in the nation. We had taken extreme care on the advice of the pastors, who were eager to protect both us and the church from difficulties. Contrary to past years, we had stayed in the hotel, spoken with the pastors standing alongside us and not taken control of the meetings, always seeking to give the appearance that they were in control.

Hurriedly, we ran down the stairs and up the black streets to the church, praying that God would keep us safe.

We banged and shouted at the locked gate, and finally, Hosea came!

"What is wrong?" he said as he had farewelled us just a short time before! We thrust the note into his hands and fell into the chairs! Concerned, he read the summons. "We will come with you. I will organise this! Be ready at 9:30 a.m., and we will get you."

"What about the service?" we asked.

"I will tell the pastor," he said.

We prayed and left.

The next day at 10:00 a.m., with our interpreter and the three senior pastors of the Assemblies of God, we presented ourselves to the head of immigration while praying earnestly. An unidentified suburban house held the office. They asked the pastors to sit in an exterior room and ushered us into an interior office.

The official thanked us for coming and said he had been to the hotel many times to look for us, but we were never there. He told us we left at 7:00 a.m. and did not return until midnight or after. He said, "Please speak up, I am a little deaf, and I can't speak any English!"

This statement, for two purposes, sought to mislead us into revealing vital information, to think he did not understand what we were saying and to allow the hidden taping of our conversation from the back room! The interpreter, though, knew the man and knew he spoke English.

"He speaks English," she quietly warned me.

God had told me before I left New Zealand, "When you are called before authorities, governors, and rulers, be as wise as a serpent and as harmless as a dove!"

We arrived at the interview believing God would be with us, and he answered. Several foreign visitors had recently been deported from this area for doing the things we were doing—preaching, testifying, ministering, and visiting homes. We had been aware that people were watching and reporting on what we were doing. That same morning, a gravely concerned senior pastor had discussed with us whether we should cut our visit short and move on from the area.

This man examined our passports. "You have tourist visas, but you are doing no tourist activities," he said. The interpreter and I both replied, disclaiming this. "You are only visiting churches," he said, "and travelling in private cars."

Careful to tell him nothing new, I said, "You know I have been here before?" He nodded, and I continued, "Well, these people are my friends. Isn't it logical that they would want for me to visit and I would travel with them?" He remained silent when we reminded him, "There is no public transport, so this is the only way we can travel." It is now forbidden for foreigners to travel in private cars!

"Where have you been? What churches have you visited?" he asked.

Again, even more careful, I named the places he would have expected and especially the churches connected with the pastors listening through the open door. Carefully, I omitted the church from the night before, knowing he would be unaware of it.

He said, "I am not warning you, just wanting to talk to you, you must not be the focus of attention in a meeting." He told us he had an open door any time if we had questions and not to hesitate to come and talk to him. He knew where we usually came from and where we were going on to.

Praise God for our NZ status and the favor God gave us, as had we been Americans or Puerto Ricans, they would have expelled us. The officer said we were to have no public ministry.

Finally, I asked him, "You know these people are my friends, and when I go to the meetings, they want me to pray for them. What shall I do?"

"That's okay," he said. "You can pray for them." He said goodbye to us, and we left to continue doing everything we had done before, and in fact, we got bolder. The gear changed, and we moved faster with greater speed to continue the safety of the drive!

They frequently spoke of fire in the Bible. We have spoken earlier of Abraham and the fire and Moses with the fire. Moses looked upon the glory (Exodus 3) at the burning bush and on the mountain. And now we want to look at Isaiah 6, where Isaiah had an experience of the fire. The fire released and releases the glory. People throughout the Bible beheld the glory. Now on this significant year, when the king, his cousin, died, he glimpses the Lord; he looks into the heavenly realm.

Isaiah 6 tells us that God got Isaiah's attention. The angel took the fiery coal and placed on Isaiah's lips. This brought change, challenge, choice, and costly consecration. This finished his old life.

Isaiah 6:1-8 (ESV), "In the year that King Uzziah died, I saw the Lord sitting on a throne, high and lifted up, and the train of His robe filled the temple" (John 12.41). Isaiah saw the glory of Jesus and spoke of Him. Above it stood seraphim; each one had six wings: with two he covered his face, with two he covered his feet, and with two he flew." "And one cried to another and said: "Holy, holy, holy is the LORD of hosts; The whole earth is full of His glory!" "And the posts of the door were shaken by the voice of him who cried out, and the house was filled with smoke" So I said: "Woe is me, for I am undone! Because I am a man of unclean lips, And I dwell in the midst of a people of unclean lips; For my eyes have seen the King, The LORD of hosts." "Then one of the seraphim flew to me, haying in his hand a live coal which he had taken with the tongs from the altar." "And he touched my mouth with it, and said: "Behold, this has touched your lips; Your iniquity is taken away, and your sin purged. Also I heard the voice of the Lord, saying: "Whom shall I send, And who will go for Us?" Then I said, "Here am I! Send me." And He said, "Go, and tell this people: 'Keep on hearing, but do not understand; Keep on seeing, but do not perceive.'"

Isaiah had a supernatural encounter. Not only did he look upon Jesus, but he also gazed at the seraphim, the fiery angels, as they flew crying, "Holy, holy, holy." He looked into the heavenly realm, he glimpsed the glory, and it changed him forever. The vision utterly redirected, reformed, and transformed his life and ministry. It's the same for us! Isaiah gazed at three dimensions. There are many areas in the scriptures that deal with three dimensions. God blessed him, God broke him, and God gave him to the world.

This is a vision of Father, Son, and Holy Spirit. Three dimensions, a word of woe, a word of confession, lo a word of cleansing, go a word of commission. This an upward vision he looked at the Lord, this an inward vision he glimpsed himself, this an outward vision he gazed at the world! Can you catch the connections here? In a vision of height, he beheld the Lord high and lifted up. In a vision of depth, he inspected the recesses of his own heart. In a vision of breadth, he scrutinised the world!

He looked at a vision of holiness, a vision of hellishness, and a vision of hopelessness. I am undone and unclean. All implied by the words, who will go for us

God came in the darkness and revealed his glory. When he comes, he always reveals his glory, and we are never the same again. Without him, there is only darkness in our lives. I prayed over hundreds of people in Cuba that they would behold his glory.

The coal of fire touched his lips, purifying them.

This is a baptism of fire! In the theology of holiness, we like to think of the fire coming to Isaiah, bringing consecration, separation from sin, separation from the world, but we only have half the picture! There is a separation to serve! We are set apart, a peculiar people special to God.

In 1 Peter 2:9 (ESV), it says we are to declare the praises of him who called us out of darkness into his glorious light.

God wants to touch our lives with the fire of the Holy Spirit, burning out the rubbish to make us like gold. Gold melts in the fire! People in

Cuba said fire burnt into their bodies, and the result is obedience. When God the Holy Spirit comes to us, he purifies us, and all we want to do is obey to do what he tells us. And what does he tell us to do? God says, whom shall I send? Isaiah's response came, "Here I am, send me." What is our response? Says then shallWe must study the word and respond!

Acts 1:8 (ESV) speaks of the baptism of fire, the fire that fills our lives, changes us, challenges us, breaks us, and sends us to the world! We have to give away the fire, or else, soon the fire in our lives will go out! We are to be on fire and burning with the spirit.

When people are touched by the fire, it's not pleasant, it's not comfortable. They scream, yell, roll on the floor. They testified that the fire burnt them from the inside out. The fire brought Isaiah fresh revelations. He glimpsed Jesus; he gazed into the glory. People caught sight of angels. They notice fire on our heads, lightning in the building. They experience the glory.

Can the Holy Spirit trust us? He will not trust us with his power unless we have a surrendered life, except a grain of wheat fall to the ground and die—total surrender. The coal of fire touched his lips, purifying them.

In our meetings, we have seen the fire fall. In Russia, when we travelled to the camp meeting, the pastor's sister sitting well back in the meeting wept. I watched her with concern.

"Call the people to repent, call the people to repentance," the Holy Spirit said.

"God is calling, God is speaking. Do you have sin in your life? It's time to repent," I cried. "God is grieved with your lives. He wants clean, holy lives. Turn to him, turn from your sin. Are your attitudes and actions wrong? Clean up your lives. The Lord is saying tell him you are sorry and will change."

I heard loud sobbing throughout the large room. They played the powerful song from the Pensacola revival. "I'm running, I'm running, I'm running to the mercy seat where Jesus, where Jesus answers prayer. I'm running, I'm running, and they came running, crying, wailing!"

About a third of those assembled knelt at the front in humility and repentance. Some were wailing, everyone sobbing with deep weeping from their inner being. A somber, sober time. We were crying out to God as we reviewed our lives, confessing aloud wrong attitudes and actions, lack of devotion to Jesus and the word.

There had been an exceptional time of the presence of God during the worship and testimonies from the previous day. A child had shared a vision of God, and as he did, his face shone with the glory. God had revealed himself as three immense balls of fire to this ten-year-old boy while he lay on the floor under the power of God.

"Don't grieve the Holy Spirit," I cried. Tears rolled down my cheeks. "He is here. He is grieving for you. He wants your entire lives. Turn to him. Tell him you're sorry. Confess your sin. Just as the coal touched Isaiah's lips, and so painful, he changed, he cried out to God. We are unworthy, we are unworthy."

Some more came, some gathered with others, God moved among us. It changed lives. It changed us. My first experience of such a move of God, and even as I write, I feel the call and cry to repent. It stirs within me. This powerful movement of the Holy Spirit brought conviction and desire to change. Reader, do you want to change? Do you want more of the precious Holy Spirit? Do you want the fire to touch your life?

Allow the Holy Spirit to convict you and bring you to repentance. Yield to him. He is here just as he moved in Russia, and he wants *you*—ALL OF YOU. He will not force you. He is a gentleman. He is grieving for you to yield more of your life to him. He is grieving over you and me. He wants us to have holy lives.

This camp meeting had been wonderful. Before the meeting, the pastor said, "We will do whatever the Holy Spirit wants and give him space to move."

Because of this, as we allowed the Holy Spirit to draw us into intimacy during the worship, with no sermon, the presence of God increased in the assembly.

RUSSIA CAMP MEETING

CHILD WHO SAW THE GLORY RUSSIA CAMP MEETING

RUSSIA ON THE BUS

The Holy Spirit is the gift Jesus gave his disciples (John 20:22 ESV). God is at work in the believer's life and in the world. Because the Holy Spirit is God's presence in the believer's life and in the world, there is a revelation of sin and God's judgement. A revelation comes of being righteous in God's presence (John 16:8 ESV). The presence of God's spirit brings the overwhelming sense of one's uncleanness and the overwhelming desire to be clean.

The statement "He shall baptise you with the Holy Ghost, and with fire" means that Jesus immerses (baptises) people in the presence of God so they are aware of their sin and the need to be cleansed. To be baptised with the Holy Spirit and fire is to be convicted concerning sin and righteousness and judgement (John 16:8 ESV).

To be baptised with the Holy Spirit has a wider application than this, but when the Holy Spirit is coupled with fire (as in the phrase in Matthew 3:11, Luke 3:16 ESV), the particular aspect of the Holy Spirit's work as described here is in view (Phil Logan *Holman Bible Dictionary*).

When the fire comes, it touches and changes our lives. That happened in Russia, Sikkim, and Cuba, when the fire fell.

There are two sides to the fire: glory and judgement. Glory brings revelation of God and his word, relationship with Jesus, worship and glory. Judgement brings repentance and purity.

We should consider four things about the fire. It brings us into relationship, leads us on, is painful and costly, and brings the glory.

This another amazing trip to Cuba, accompanied by a lady from Wanganui, New Zealand, we witnessed God moving with significant power. From day 1, when the airline left two of our bags in Mexico, God protected us. When these bags were delivered to us, it came in one box, which had been inspected and almost opened. It would have ensured our immediate expulsion from the country, as unknown to us, it contained much incriminating literature. Bibles for delivery had testimonies from believers in restricted persecuted nations with some from Cuba and an emblem identifying an organisation forbidden in Cuba. Once again, we praised God for the miracle of looking after us!

GIVING PRECIOUS BIBLES TO SENIOR PASTORS

When the fire comes, it causes challenges, change, choices, and consecration. The fire is painful and costly, but it always leads us on. The fire of God is present in the nations today.

REVIVAL FIRES ARE OFTEN FIRES OF PERSECUTION

The letter read, "Cajo babo is gone! Bulldozed by the Cuban Government just two weeks after your visit to the church. Not a sign is left!" During our ministry there, we had felt an impending sense of danger to us and to the church because of our presence. The church filled, and many people crowded outside, trying to look in. We noticed a new awareness of evil because of the many unbelievers present and the tremendous demonic opposition. For the past year, the government had been threatening these believers with the closure of the work.

"Are you going to fight us like the others did?" the police asked the pastor of another church.

"No!" he replied. "You are not fighting me, you are fighting God!"

The police had come with bulldozers to tear the church down and destroy the buildings! The policeman stepped back, taken by surprise at the reply. He just stood there, thought for a few moments, and then they ordered the bulldozers and police to leave. They left, never to return. It saved this church through the wisdom and prompting of the Holy Spirit. Jesus is victorious. Churches and house churches have been closed, pastors imprisoned, but souls are being added daily to the church throughout the nation. The fire of persecution has been fueled by the government of Cuba because of burgeoning church growth and actions by the United States.

Police showed great consternation and anger when they came to bulldoze yet another church. The entire neighbourhood and everything they owned met them! The streets around the church were covered and blocked with furniture and belongings. They put everything out of the houses on the road accessing the church, and the people were angry and protesting. The neighbours greeted the policemen, "Bulldoze our houses too! If you destroy the church, we don't want to live here anymore!"

Stunned, police went away angrily, saying," The church put them up to it!"

The church didn't do it; God did.

Daniel 3 tells us of a release of the supernatural came while they were in the fire. In Daniel 3:22-24 (ESV), the fire slew the men who carried out the king's orders against Shadrach, Meshach, and Abednigo. With the fire came the release of the supernatural. Four men were seen and one like as unto the Son of Man.

We were at an overnight retreat for pastors and evangelists. The previous night's meeting had been difficult. Contrary to what we had been told, the doors and windows were open. They had invited the whole church, a public meeting!

"You've forgotten how to fight! Witchcraft has risen. This is not the Cuba you knew a year ago. You have been listening to us and the government and stopped listening to the Holy Spirit!" the senior pastor challenged me.

The interpreter turned on me and said, "Yes, you have, you have got frightened and stopped listening to the Holy Spirit!"

"You brought the word of the Lord, and then you sat down and did nothing about it! How could you do that?" the pastor admonished.

My mouth opened and shut like a fish. It stunned me. "How have I forgotten?" I asked. "I'm not in charge. You are!" I said. "I couldn't take over. You have the programme!"

"That's just it," he said. "You are not in charge because you are not doing what the Holy Spirit wants! We are Pentecostals here, and you brought the word of the Lord. God had given me the same word, yet you brought it, but you did nothing about it!"

We were at the back of the building, having a private conversation, three of us, the senior pastor, the interpreter, and me.

As foreigners with tourist visas, they forbade us to preach, but we could share and minister if people wanted us to pray for them. We had shared and moved along the rows, praying for the people. Terrible, with no anointing of the Holy Spirit, and very difficult clambering through the narrow rows past the people, the atmosphere seemed tense, and I cried out to God, weeping and saying to the Lord, "Lord, if this is the new Cuba, it's too hard! I can't do it anymore!"

When I finished praying for the people, I cried and retreated to an area outside. There, God spoke and said to me, "Go back in!"

Reluctantly, I returned to find the senior pastor had taken control as he broke powers and sought the presence of God. The next morning we rose for the early morning prayer meeting, but very few attended. The morning programme started at seven thirty, and the day's details were given, but they were busy talking, talking, talking. These leaders, evangelists and pastors, were suffering from restriction and persecution. The Holy Spirit moved prophetically, most wonderfully, bringing much healing, renewal, and restoration.

CUBA

What an unforgettable Christmas Day we had in Cuba that year when the brother of the senior pastor came back to Jesus after ten years of backsliding. The families were weeping, as Satan tried to block the translation of the word, which helped to call him back. God broke through, and he bowed his knee to Jesus! How we rejoiced to see this sinner restored to the Lord. Millions are in the valley of decision. Who will tell them of Jesus's love?

Nothing can hinder us from being accepted; there is nothing between when God forgives our sin and washes us clean. Exodus 13:21 (ESV) tell us the Lord led before in a pillar of fire. They wasted no time, day and night. When we are in the fire, we are in his time. Never left alone, they were always in the presence. They walked in the presence. Do we?

Before one trip to Cuba, there were many visions and prophetic words about fire. A man shared at the church meeting where he prayed for me, "I glimpse flaming arrows going before you. Everywhere they land, fires are lit. Until throughout the island, fires are burning."

I spoke on the fire of God to this conservative Pentecostal church Bible school in Yangon, where the ladies wore headscarves and no jewellery during the services. The fire fell, and with the fire came the glory. Everyone on the floor cried out to God in repentance. The spirit of the Lord moved, bringing healing to a young woman who screamed and writhed on the floor. This girl had been thrown out of her family, beaten and told they never wanted to catch sight of her again because of her stand as a Christian. That night God came and touched and transformed her life. At the end of this precious time in the presence of the Lord, we sang that beautiful song, "Alleluia, Alleluia," and worshipped the Lord.

The pastor, who had been among those crying out to God, said, "I knew I had to repent, but I did not know what for."

He thanked us for coming and said if we had come only for the young woman, it would have been enough, but everyone had changed.

There are aspects to revelation, revelation of God, revelation of ourselves.

Revelation of God. Exodus 3:2 (ESV) tells us the angel appeared in a flame. What Moses gazed upon caused him to act. He looked, he took off his shoes, and he worshipped. God revealed himself to him, a supernatural revelation. This revelation got his attention. This is the hour of the burning bush; God wants to meet with us and get our attention. It's time for us to meet with God. We leave the old life at the fire.

In Exodus 3:5 (ESV), the angel says, "Don't come any closer!" Yet the Bible speaks of intimacy. God declared his identity. Moses had to die; he had to go God's way in everything to become an instrument in God's hands. There is no hope otherwise. We must learn this lesson. If we learn, there is no limit to what God can do through us. This became a new day for Moses. He'd tried the old way, his way. As it didn't work, it brought failure. There are many examples of the fire in the scriptures.

In Ezekiel 1:4-13, 27 (ESV), the fire revealed the glory of God. The lightning, bright, making him shine like fire (Ezekiel 8:2 ESV).

Revelation 19:12 (ESV) His feet were as fire, burning out the path (Revelation 10:1 ESV).

I heard a story about a church, where the firemen came. There had been a call, a report of a fire in the church, flames coming out the windows. But they could not find the fire! They checked everything and could not explain why it appeared. They noticed a fire, but they could not put it out! At the time the people were praying at the church prayer meeting.

THE GLORY

"I saw the glory, the glory of God was here," he said.

I listened carefully and said, "What do you mean? What did you see?"

"It was like the glory described in the transfiguration when Moses and Elijah were there with Jesus and the disciples saw the brightness."

"What did you see?" I asked.

"You were ministering at the front of the church, and all around you was glorious white light it bathed you in the glory," he said. "It was an utterly incredible experience. The light was so bright it was like the Bible says that Peter and the disciples saw, like brilliant sunlight which you could not look into! I had to cover my eyes! The presence of God was so wonderful."

This pastor had called in briefly at the church that morning to tell us about his wife's accident and had this experience of God.

God's glory refers to the weight or influence he carries in the universe and to the overwhelming brilliance when he appears to people (Exodus 16:7-10, Isaiah 6:3, Ephesians 1:12-17, Hebrews 1:3 ESV). It is his presence in all his sovereign power, righteousness, and love. Sometimes the Bible describes the glory of God as a physical manifestation. Sometimes it is a spiritual perception, as in a sense of tremendous awe before God. We see the glory of God when we are deeply impressed with a sense of his presence and power. It is when heaven touches earth and manifests. We have seen the glory manifest in our conferences across the world.

It's when God moves powerfully. We were in Central Myanmar with our precious Brother Lahtoi, a group of us ministering to one hundred students and forty children in the glory. All the children, orphans, were weeping on the platform for two hours and the students laughing, crying, as the glory hit them, and they were rolling in the dirt. The Holy Spirit blasted them. Just as Jesus brought the glory when he brought heaven to earth, he expressed heaven here on earth. The conditions of heaven, he brought to earth. When he ministered and raised the dead, he brought healing, deliverance, and at the transfiguration, heaven touched earth. He said the kingdom of heaven is here, and it was, as the glory of God was manifest here on earth.

TRAINING TEAM (KEVIN TOOK THE PHOTO)
DOT, JAMES, ELISABETH, DENISE AND NONA

Heaven touched children in Baire as they sank to the floor when prayed for and saw the heavenly realm. Heaven came to the church roof when it touched a boy in the children's programme in Guantanamo. He glimpsed the ladder going up to heaven, Jacob's ladder, where he climbed up the steps with the angels going up and down. When he got to the top, he observed the glory and beauty of heaven. As he looked down over the side, he looked into hell and gazed at the flames, the fires, the smoke. His life changed as he saw the glory.

CHILD IN CUBA WHO SAW THE GLORY

A young woman in front of me was kneeling on the floor, crying, as in a trance. If I had waved my hand in front of her, she would not have responded. As she spoke to Jesus, she hugged and kissed him. What a beautiful experience to watch. Her face shone as the glory of

God manifested all over her. And as I watched, she talked, she kissed, she hugged, and no one was there, just me directly in front of her. So amazing as I glimpsed Jesus touch her. It was beautiful. He took her to a garden with flowers, beautiful flowers, brilliant colours, and gave her the flowers. Wonderful, beyond what you could imagine, ask, or think! Would you like to receive flowers in heaven? That's what people are getting when the glory comes. Everywhere men have received flowers, women have received flowers. So beautiful, Jesus gave us flowers. When the glory comes, it touches and changes lives. When she woke up, a translator said to me she's been in heaven, she's been with Jesus. Get her to give away what she got, get her to give away the flowers. We did, and she did!

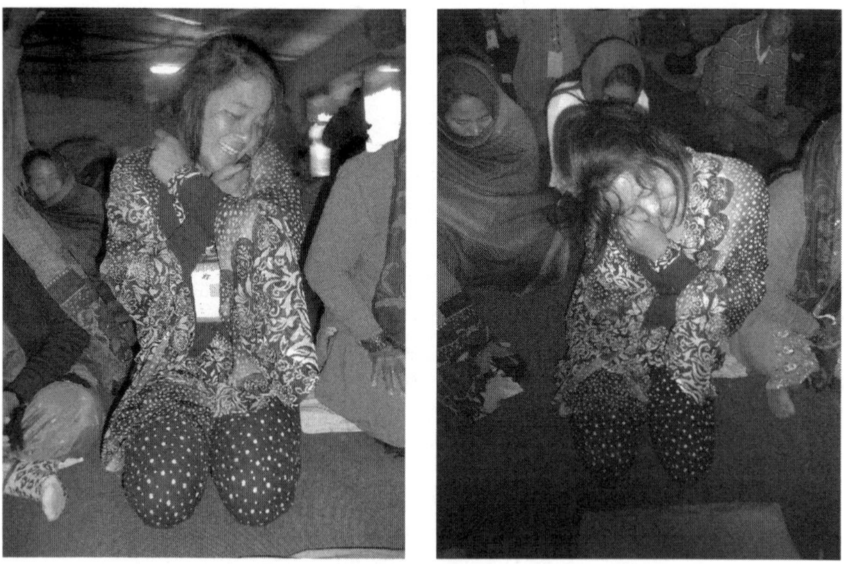

YOUNG WOMAN IN NEPAL RECEIVING THE FLOWERS FROM HEAVEN

A young woman in Myktina shone with the glory as she cried, and she shared she had a revelation of Jesus and he told her he loved her. Another man danced with Jesus and was hugged by him! Others experienced his love and saw the glories of heaven, not visions, but reality. In experiences before our eyes, God released his glory.

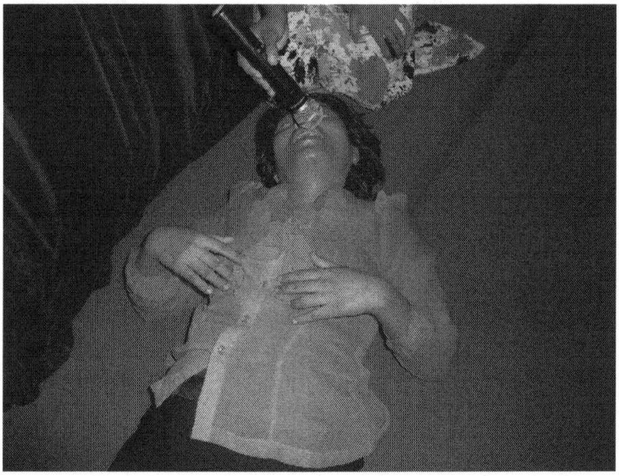

MYANMAR

We can release the glory by faith, as we declare and decree that fire is here, and release the fire as it comes. By faith, we release water, the water of the springs of life, the life of the Holy Spirit, the fragrances, the power, the miracles, the power of God, the healings, the boldness, the authority—all aspects of the glory!

Glory is the weighty importance and shining majesty that accompanies God's presence. The basic meaning of the Hebrew word *kabod* is heavy. Glory is, thus, that side of God that humans recognise and to which humans respond in confession, worship, and praise (*Holman Bible Dictionary*).

Numbers 14:21 (ESV), "but truly, as I live, all the earth shall be filled with the glory of the LORD." (Isaiah 6:3).

> Be exalted, O God, above the heavens;
> Let Your glory be above all the earth.
> (—Psalm 57:11 ESV)

We are carriers of his glory to bring that glory over all the earth.

There are choices made to have the glory. In Psalm 8:4–5, in the beginning, man was clothed with this glory. Clothed and crowned with the presence of God, with the same fire and flame and beauty, they shone like God shines. A shimmering force field of glory surrounded and protected them because God made man in his image, clothed in his glory. When they sinned, they knew it left, for they lost the covering, and they were naked and ashamed (Genesis 1-3). In Genesis 3, they exchanged and lost their glory, the wealth of God, the heavyweight of the glory, as God is heavy with everything you could ever want or need.

> For all have sinned and fall short of the glory of God but when we are born again, clothed with his glory we return to that rightful position where the glory of God comes upon us Jesus dwells in us, and we receive again that glory lost at the fall.
> (—Romans 3:23 ESV)

Think on that. We are clothed with his glory. Because we were born again, we were restored to the image of God.

FEATURES OF THE GLORY

The glory is active; it moves.

In Ezekiel 10:4 (ESV), it tells us the glory went up, it paused, it filled, it consumed, it stood over, and it covered.

Habakkuk 3:4 (ESV tell us his brightness was like the light, rays flashed from his hand, and there he veiled his power.

Another rendering of this verse in keeping with other prophets statements is "His brightness was like the brightest light, the brilliance of God's glory; rays streamed from His hand; and there in the sun like splendour was the hiding place of his power." The glory was in the midst. My grandson saw this glory and expressed it as white brilliant shimmering light. We can experience and see the glory.

It is light. God shines forth brilliantly. It thunders and comes as smoke. Ezekiel 1:27-28 (ESV) speaks of a halo around him. It filled the court with the radiance and brightness, the cloud of the Lord's glory (Isaiah 60:19, Isaiah 6 ESV).

There is the cloud of fire.

> Now it came to pass, as Aaron spoke to the whole congregation of the children of Israel, that they

> looked towards the wilderness, and behold, the glory of the LORD appeared in the cloud.
> (—Exodus 16:10 ESV)

> Now the glory of the LORD rested on Mount Sinai, and the cloud covered it six days. And on the seventh day He called to Moses out of the midst of the cloud. The sight of the glory of the LORD was like a consuming fire on the top of the mountain in the eyes of the children of Israel.
> (—Exodus 24:16-17 ESV)

> Then the cloud covered the tabernacle of meeting, and the glory of the LORD filled the tabernacle. And Moses was not able to enter the tabernacle of meeting, because the cloud rested above it, and the glory of the LORD filled the tabernacle.
> (—Exodus 40:34-35 ESV)

Wind, the wind of God, the fullness is called the glory. The smoke of God is called the glory Isaiah 4:5, … a cloud and smoke by day and the shining of a flaming fire by night. Over all the glory, there will be a covering. There came a defence of divine love and protection.

Revelation 15:8 (ESV) tell us that the temple was filled with smoke from the glory of God and from his power, and no one could enter the temple.

In the actions of the glory, the glory appeared to all, and it brought challenge, choice, change, and consecration as with Isaiah.

They beheld, saw the glory, and heard the voice of God.

> And you said: "Surely the LORD our God has shown us His glory and His greatness, and we have heard

> His voice from the midst of the fire. We have seen this day that God speaks with man; yet he still lives."
> (—Deuteronomy 5:24 ESV)

> The word became flesh and dwelt among us, and we beheld His glory.
> (—John 1:14 ESV)

2 Chronicles 7:1-2 (ESV), "When Solomon had finished praying, fire came down from heaven and consumed the burnt offering and the sacrifices; and the glory of the LORD filled the temple. And the priests could not enter the house of the LORD, because the glory of the LORD had filled the Lord's house," (Daniel 10:9, Matthew 17:6 ESV).

Revelation 1:12-18 (ESV) verse 17, he (John) fell down as the dead, he saw Jesus and His face was like the sun shining in brilliance and full power as at midday.

> The city had no need of the sun or of the moon to shine in it, for the glory of God illuminated it The Lamb is its light.
> (—Revelation 21:23 ESV)

> It shone with the glory of God, and its brilliance was like that of a very precious jewel, like a jasper, clear as crystal.
> (—Revelation 21:11 ESV)

When the glory came, fear came. They fell on their faces. An American missionary to the Mexican Indians for over thirty years tells the story of when the glory came to his churches. They could not stand for four days. They all just lay on the ground. He looked around for elders to pray with the people, and they were no use as they were lying under the power of God!

In Daniel 10, Daniel trembled with fear when the glory came.

The prophet told the senior pastor, "I'll be all finished by twelve, midday, Sunday."

The man had come to the growing church at a critical time of control, division, and dissension by six families. The weekend meetings were almost uneventful. Sunday came. The service was almost finished when people came running into the church from all over the suburb. They were weeping and crying out to God in repentance. Each of the six young men came in repentance, and within weeks, God had moved each family away from the church. The people said the Holy Spirit had come upon them in their homes, and as they walked on the streets, compelling them to go immediately to the church, compelling them to repent, compelling them to change.

> And behold, an angel of the Lord stood before them, and the glory of the Lord shone around them, and they were greatly afraid.
> (—Luke 2:9 ESV)

Ezekiel 1:28 (ESV), "Like the appearance of a rainbow in a cloud on a rainy day, so was the appearance of the brightness all around it. This was the appearance of the likeness of the glory of the LORD. So when I saw it, I fell on my face, and I heard a voice of One speaking" (Revelation 4:3 ESV) When the glory came, the spirit entered him and brought new direction.

> And the cherubim lifted their wings and mounted up from the earth in my sight. When they went out, the wheels were beside them; and they stood at the door of the east gate of the Lord's house, and the glory of the God of Israel was above them. The Spirit lifted him up, brought revelation.
> (—Ezekiel 10:19 ESV)

Ezekiel 11:22-24 (ESV), "So the cherubim lifted up their wings, with the wheels beside them, and the glory of the God of Israel was high above them. And the glory of the LORD went up from the midst of the city and stood on the mountain, which is on the east side of the city. Then the Spirit took me up and brought me in a vision by the Spirit of God into Chaldea, to those in captivity.

Ezekiel 43:2 (ESV), "And behold, the glory of the God of Israel came from the way of the east. His voice was like the sound of many waters; and the earth shone with His glory. It was like the appearance of the vision which I saw; like the vision which I saw when I came to destroy the city. The visions were like the vision which I saw by the River Chebar; and I fell on my face. And the glory of tire LORD came into the temple by way of the gate which faces towards the east. The Spirit lifted me up and brought me into the inner court; and behold, the glory of the LORD filled the temple."

There is no glory except the way of the cross. When there is a revelation of the cross, there is a revelation of the glory.

> Truly, truly, I say to you, unless a grain of wheat falls into the earth and dies, it remains alone; but if it dies, it bears much fruit.
> (—John 12:24 ESV)

Whoever loves his life loses it, and whoever hates his life in this world will keep it for eternal life. If anyone serves me, he must follow me; and where I am, there will my servant be also. If anyone serves me, the Father will honour him. There is the challenge, the choice, the change, and the consecration of the cross.

> And he said to all, "If anyone would come after me, let him deny himself and take up his cross daily and follow me. For whoever would save his life will lose it, but whoever loses his life for my sake will save it.

> For what does it profit a man if he gains the whole world and loses or forfeits himself? For whoever is ashamed of me and of my words, of him will the Son of Man be ashamed when he comes in his glory and the glory of the Father and of the holy angels."
> (—Luke 9:23-26 ESV)

> When the Son of Man comes in His glory-majesty-splendour, and all the holy angels with Him, then He will sit on the throne of His glory.
> (—Matthew 25:31 ESV)

We know that one day he is coming in glory to take us to rule and reign with him. Until then, as carriers of that glory, we recognise we bring the glory wherever we go. From our citizenship in heaven, we rule and reign with him, bringing heaven to earth.

> Then they will see the Son of Man coming in a cloud with power and great glory.
> (—Luke 21:27 ESV)

The Son of Man will come to rule and reign. He comes from the cross to the throne, from the suffering to the glory. He will come with power and great glory. We too come from the cross to rule and reign as kings and priests.

Our responsibility is we must rise to the challenge, make the right choices to change and consecrate our lives as we declare his glory among the nations, his wonders among all peoples (Psalm 96:3 ESV) We are to be carriers of the glory, to bring his glory everywhere as we bring heaven to earth.

Ephesians 1:12-17 (ESV); "We are destined & appointed to live for the praise of His Glory."

Isaiah 58:8 (ESV) says then shall your light break forth like the dawn, and your healing shall spring up speedily; your righteousness shall go before you; the glory of the LORD shall be your rear guard.

> Arise, shine; For your light has come! And the glory of the LORD is risen upon you. (—Isaiah 60:1 ESV)

Isaiah 62:3 (ESV), "You shall also be a crown of glory in the hand of the LORD, and a royal diadem in the hand of your God. -beautiful & prosperous. God's glory will arise upon us, we will be carriers of His glory. His glory will be seen in us.

It had been an interesting meeting in a very poor gypsy area on the outskirts of Bourgas in Bulgaria. The church was in the middle of a large compound, and there was no microphone. They said they wished the people outside would listen, but they shut the door! In answer to prayer, it reopened. As I spoke, noisy children came in and out at the back. An old man got up noisily and shooed them out! At the same time, a very violent man at the front kept getting up from where he was sitting, rushing across the room and thumping people!

When ministry time came, the people crowded in from outside and pushed us further and further back. They pushed around, gazing at what was happening and wanting to touch us. It soon became impossible to minister as it became dangerous. The leaders feared there would be a riot, and the meeting closed.

With the door locked and bolted, people shouted to be let in. And they peered in the barred windows. The power of God came, and so had the near riot! After we farewelled, all the people returned to the room; we allowed only a few into the church at a time. The wonderful presence of God came, and the Holy Spirit moved both in power and prophetically. Gradually, the room filled up as more and more people were admitted, and it once again became dangerous. We escaped to the apartment building close by, where we stayed the night with the pastor and his family.

At Dimitrogad, a woman testified that her three-year-old grandchild had been deaf and dumb and crippled. Some days after we prayed, he heard and spoke, and today the child is totally healed of all conditions.

DIMITROGRAD, BULGARIA

The prophetic word in Cuba said a fiery cross across Bulgaria and Turkey, and the pastors said I would see a move of God like I had evidenced in Cuba! In Shumen, it happened. The people shouted and pointed to a woman on the floor who had been anointed with oil. We were astounded to find the oil on her head blood red in the sign of a cross. That morning, in Varna, the pastor brought out his shirt to show us, and all over this white shirt were twenty-four black crosses! This a trip of signs and wonders and miracles.

The glory of God refers to the supernatural life and essence of God, the very power that makes him God.

In Darjeeling, in this cold operatic theatre building, there was snow outside. A freezing day in this mountainous place, we were below the platform. The glory fell, and the people fell, in a stack one on top of the other. Just amazing as they didn't seem to get hurt, they were all bodies on top of one another as the power of God filled them, as the glory of God came in that miserable cold place. But when the glory comes, the fire comes, so no one was cold.

DARJEELING THEATRE

We are to expect the glory. We can live a life so powerful. It exceeds anything we could ever ask or think, a life full of the fiery brightness of God. We are not poor beggars trudging through the heat and cold! We are to expect the glorious to happen to us. We are to have hope, earnest expectation, a joyful anticipation of good, a strained expectancy and eager longing. This expectation is to absorb all our attentions! Our life is to be supernatural, filled with glory as we bring heaven to earth.

> Faith is the substance of things hoped for, the evidence of things not seen.
> (—Hebrews 11:1 ESV)

GOD'S WORD + HOPE + FAITH = MANIFESTATIONS

This spiritual process always works the same way; hope forms the image according to the word, then faith rises and gives substance to that image, making it a reality in the natural physical realm. What are we to be hoping for? Healing, financial success, new house, car?

Romans 5:I-2 (ESV), "We rejoice in the hope of the glory of God." We are to expect the glory, not just these other things, but also the glory. We are to expect the manifest presence of God, the very presence of God, to rise in us so powerfully, that instead of believing for these things, we walk in them by faith every day. When we expect the glory, we live like we really are a joint heir with Jesus who was crowned with glory and honour.

> For You have made him a little lower than the angels,
> And You have crowned him with glory and honour.
> (—Psalm 8:5 ESV)

Jesus is the revelation of the glory.

> The Son is the radiance of God's glory and the exact representation of his being, sustaining all things by his powerful word. After he had provided purification for sins, he sat down at the right hand of the Majesty in heaven.
> (—Hebrews 1:3 ESV)

Hebrews 2:7-9 (ESV), "You have made him a little lower than the angels; You have crowned him with glory and honour, And set him over the works of Your hands. "But we see Jesus, who was made a little lower than the angels, for the suffering of death crowned with glory and honour, that He, by the grace of God, might taste death for everyone."

In 2 Corinthians 3:1 8 (TPT), it says we can all draw close to him with the veil removed from our faces. And with no veil, we all become like mirrors that brightly reflect the glory of the Lord *Jesus.* We are being transfigured into his very image as we move from one brighter level of glory to another. And this glorious transfiguration comes from the Lord, who is the spirit.

We are constantly being transfigured. This brings its challenge, choices, change, and consecration.

Acts 9: 1-4 and Acts 26:12–19 (ESV) tell us that Paul had the challenge of Stephen. He observed Stephen have a revelation of the glory. This faced Paul with the challenge, the choice, the change, and the consecration that the glory brought. As the glory was brilliant and revelational, it changed the world that Paul lived in forever. When we yield to the spirit of God, the glory changes our world forever.

> Stephen said, "Brethren and fathers, listen: The God of glory appeared to our father Abraham when he was in Mesopotamia, before he dwelt in Haran . . ."
> (—Acts 7:2 ESV)

> But he, being full of the Holy Spirit, controlled by Him gazed into heaven and saw the glory-splendour and majesty of God, and Jesus standing at the right hand of God . . ."
> (—Acts 7:55 ESV)

Paul became a carrier of the glory. We are all to be carriers of the glory.

It was chaotic. They laughed, shouted, cried, all drunk sprawled on the floor! The people from outside were peering in the window in amazement and pointing at what was happening. This is the ground floor of the hotel reception area! A worker at the hotel came to the door, looked around her, and quickly ran in, shutting the door behind her.

Within seconds, she joined the others on the floor. Two men inside the room watched with concerned interest. It was their turn next. I turned towards them, and they fled! A tall young man was watching from outside with interest.

"Would you like us to pray for you?" I asked. He nodded and stood against the door inside the room. As I prayed, he watched, and he slid down the door gently to the floor. I asked him if he knew Jesus.

"I worship Buddha," he said. "I came from Yangon this morning."

Immediately, after being touched by the power of God in this stunning way, he gave his life to Jesus.

We had met three pastors on the stairs, and they had shared with us, asking us to come to their churches. As we could not do so, they suggested we retreat into this little room and pray for them. God came with glory.

The next morning we held an impromptu revival meeting on the top floor of the hotel for the forty people who came. That's what it was—a revival! The glory came! People were baptised in the Holy Spirit and spoke in tongues. Among them was the young man from the day before who testified that he had nothing to do with Christians and never had experienced such a presence of God. He said it convinced him to follow Jesus. Two others who had come to Jesus the previous night were baptised in the Holy Spirit, along with many others. About ten or twelve were healed. It was a mighty outpouring of the Holy Spirit. We were carriers of the glory. You can be a carrier of the glory. The glory of God dwells in you.

TAUNGZALAT

Acts 26:18 (ESV) says we are chosen and sent to open the eyes of those to whom we go, so they may turn from darkness to light and from the power of Satan to God. We are to bring the word of God. We are to bring salvation that the people will receive forgiveness and release from their sins. We are appointed and anointed to serve as ministers and bear witness to Jesus, just as Paul did. What an exceptional responsibility we have.

THE SPIRITUAL ASPECTS OF THE GLORY

God gives glory.

> For the LORD God is a sun and shield; The LORD will give grace and glory; Ho good thing will He withhold From those who walk uprightly.
> (—Psalm 84:11 ESV)

In Acts 5:15 (ESV), Peter's shadow fell on the people, and it healed them. It was the field of glory around Peter. There is healing in the glory. We are to expect the glory; our expectations are to arise! We are to declare his glory among the nations.

That is what we did in Nepal. The glory came to that small group of twenty pastors and evangelists. We had taught and ministered for ten days on the principles of faith, obedience, relationship, vision, the blood, the blessings and curses, the anointing, the fire and glory of God. The final day came, and they all wanted to be baptised in the Holy Spirit. Many of the students were experienced in miracles and had seen God do amazing things yet had never experienced the in-filling of the precious Holy Spirit.

"Jesus is the baptiser in the Holy Spirit," I said. "You must seek Jesus and yield to him."

We were three ladies with the workers, who needed also to be baptised in the Holy Spirit.

We anointed the students with oil and prayed for them. It was difficult as in Nepal culture, women did not minister to men, and the only other person ministering was a Nepali woman, the wife of the leader of the work. Also, when you are ministering in a foreign nation, it's difficult to tell if the people being ministered are speaking in a new language. It was wonderful what happened. As we prayed, one man came into a very powerful, noisy tongue and fell under the power of God. We got him up speedily and took him to another man, whom he then prayed for, and the same thing happened to him. It was exciting as once we had men ministering alongside us, we had a tremendous breakthrough. The Holy Spirit fell on the whole group, and every one of them was soon speaking in an unknown language to God. The glory of God was there beautifully as the presence of God filled the room and it changed forever these leaders' lives. The New Zealand leader of the work went up to Nepal a few weeks later, and it thrilled us to hear his report.

"I saw the change," he said. "The centre will never be the same. God came in power."

It's all in the glory, our healing, our finances, everything we can ever need. It's not off in heaven waiting to come-somewhere waiting for some great anointed person to pull it down! It is in us—in you and me!

It was raining. The enormous church holding fifteen hundred people was only one third full. The air was full of expectancy and faith. The singing had been vibrant and resounding. The congregation had sung, "I surrender all, I surrender all," with much feeling. The entire congregation responded at the altar call—all five hundred of them! I sighed as the only person ministering in this big job!

People fell in all directions as I ministered to five and six at a time. The power of God astounded me. The Cubans are very good during ministry, as they always seek the Lord and pray, but tonight it's different. As a petite lady, I couldn't see a thing, unless people fell down in front of me clearing a gap. I paused, wondering what was happening, as I could hear clapping and cheering!

My eyes moved around from where I was until, finally, almost to the back of me, I saw the pastor standing on a chair. He was very excited and was waving a crutch high in the air. I recognised the man who stood beside him as the one I had prayed for a few minutes earlier. The Holy Spirit had pinned him to the floor, and when he got up, he could walk—forty years crippled, today healed.

It was like a fire in the place. Healings happened everywhere, and a man I prayed for, whose arm with contractures and a frozen shoulder, instantly healed. I lifted the arm, and it lifted with no restriction, restored! A young man delivered from suicidal demons oppressing him, gloriously set free. The glory was there. How marvelous it is to be a carrier of the glory.

HOLGUIN

> The mystery which has been hidden from ages and from generations, but now has been revealed to His saints. To them God willed to make known what are the riches of the glory of this mystery among the Gentiles: which is Christ in you, the hope of glory.
> (—Colossians 1:26-27 ESV)

2 Corinthians 4:7 (ESV), "But we have this treasure in earthen vessels, that the excellency of the power may be of God and not of us.

We are as big on the inside as all of heaven. The glory of God is in us, in you and me! How often have we thought the glory of God is going to come? No, the glory of God is within us. This glory is going to manifest when we build our hope. It will flood the earth when we meditate on the glory of God so much that faith rises and produces an image, then faith will release the glory of God from the inside of us where we can't see it to the outside where we can see it!

Remember the words Jesus spoke to Martha.

> Jesus said to her, "Did I not say to you that if you would believe you would see the glory of God?"
> (—John 11:40 ESV)

These words are just as true for us as for Martha. If we will believe for the glory, if we will meditate on the word of God until we develop our hope and expect the Glory, then faith will become the substance of it, and we will see it!

Jesus intended us to live in the glory, that sickness and disease would flee from our presence. He intended us to have a foretaste of the resurrection body here on earth. Paul wrote, that I may know him and the power of his resurrection, and may share his sufferings, becoming like him in his death, that by any means possible I may attain the resurrection from the dead.

Philippians 3:10-11 (ESV).

This is the same glory we shall go forth with it and grow in—the same glory, the cloud, the pillar of fire, the transfiguration, the power that made them fall down! We shall trample the devil until he is ashes under our feet! The glory is here. Your confession of faith and expectancy will pull it out of you. We are going to walk in that glory right in the face of hell and all it offers! Will you dare to release your expectancy of the glory?

When we pray to release the glory by faith and obedience, we declare and decree that glory. And out of our relationship with Jesus, we declare that the fire of the Holy Spirit is here, for as it comes, fire falls. When we declare the water, the refreshing spring of the Holy Spirit is here, Jesus baptises in the precious Holy Spirit. Because we release the fragrance, the smells, the sounds, they happen around us as evidence of his glory. Heaven touches earth through authority given to release, deliverances, miracles, healings, power, as we release them by faith out of our vision to see the kingdom of heaven on earth. Heaven touches earth as we move by faith to bring the glory.

Flow, Spirit. Flow into me, through me, within me, from me, out of me. River of life, flow. Spirit of God, flow. Release your power, your glory, through me! Amen. (Wigglesworth.)

SUPPLEMENTARY QUESTIONS

What are the features of the glory?

What does the statement "Without the cross, there is no glory" mean?

What happened when the glory came? What can we expect to happen when the glory comes?

How can you and I be a carrier of the glory?

CONCLUSION

In this how-to of changing gears, I have sought to encourage you to do just that. These stories are actual life experiences, not fiction, but experiences of life over years. There are still stories yet untold, maybe to come later. I want to encourage you, as this book, closes that God has a purpose for you, that purpose planned before the foundation of the world is revealed and released through his plan in your life. In this book, I have endeavored to reveal something of God's plan and purpose in all our lives. Acceleration to automatic acceleration to high speed motoring, moving in the glory and power of God. First, a question, have you given your life to Jesus Christ? Has it moved you out of neutral, out of park, to be born again? Are you moving on in God? These people I shared about have all found faith in Jesus. It's really simple. You just ask Jesus to come into your life and take away your sin. Ask him to be your Lord and Savior, to fill you with the Holy Spirit. You can do it right now.

This book would never have happened, except God stirred me to write *Heavenly Kaleidoscope*. Suddenly, unexpectedly, the time to write was here. For years, people have prophesied I needed to write books, and I said I'm too busy, as I ministered and travelled for over thirty years. Suddenly, unexpectedly, the time to write was here. As a result, I rewrote and reformatted *Endless Safari* and this one, *Changing Gears*. *Changing Gears* shows us the way forward, releases keys for us to speed up our purpose.

Because I kept extensive diaries of the events in nations since 1989, we have documented these stories. Many of these stories may have amazed you! Maybe you had never heard of heavenly experiences as written in this book or miracles or supernatural things, and I want to assure you that God is supernatural, he is real, and he wants to reveal his glory to you. Ask him to do so.

Denise has two other books recently published and available.

HEAVENLY KALEIDOSCOPE

Arm yourself with inspiration and revelation regarding the supernatural power of God. Be empowered to a new level of living as you read heavenly stories of nations and personal supernatural experiences Denise Reid has had in her walk discovering God's purpose and plan in her life. Be inspired as you taste catch a glimpse of those she has taken on teams to empower nations. You will be captured and encouraged by the experiences of the many who have received frequently changing visions and experiences to whom Denise and teams have ministered.

You will be challenged to rise to your identity as a powerful believer, as a ministry gift to the body of Christ releasing God's Kingdom on earth.

ENDLESS SAFARI

A safari is an animal adventure, into the unknown, to see and experience things you never have. Exploring new places, doing different things, experiencing constant change. An adventure into the unknown, always following a guide. You think you know what is to happen but all the time it changes. You have the ticket, you've paid the money you've received the plan. Embark with Denise on this endless journey into the unknown, encounter with her glorious experiences, and gain the trophies, of supernatural encounters in new relationships in exotic places. Be empowered to embark with a green light to move on in your own Endless Safari. Awaken your heart to the challenges facing you as you follow the guide.

Reader, are you a dreamer? When we dream, impossibilities become possibilities. When the old is revisited and the prize achieved, relationships deepen and trust in the guide becomes paramount.

Available on www.xlibris.com
You can contact Denise Reid at
denise@fourcornersministries.com **or** deniseereid@gmail.com